I0625727

Sketchy Plans & a Shot of Whiskey Copy

For the mom who loves a solid plan... and maybe something on the rocks

J.D. Evans

Curious Arrow Publishing

Published by Curious Arrow Publishing

First edition, 2025

ISBN: 979-8-9986694-0-8 (paperback) | ISBN: 979-8-9986694-2-2 (hardcover) | ISBN: 979-8-9986694-1-5 (ebook)

Disclaimer

This book is intended for informational and inspirational purposes only. The author is not a licensed therapist, counselor, or medical professional. The strategies, methods, and personal anecdotes shared throughout this book are based on personal experience and are not intended as a substitute for professional advice.

While every effort has been made to present a helpful and supportive planning system, the author makes no guarantees regarding specific results or outcomes from the use of this book or any related materials. You are responsible for your own choices, actions, and well-being.

Health & Mental Health Disclaimer

This book may touch on topics related to emotional wellness, stress, productivity, and mental load. It is not intended to diagnose, treat, or replace medical advice or mental health care. If you are struggling with your mental health, please consult with a licensed healthcare provider, therapist, or counselor.

Want to Put This Into Practice?

If you're the kind of person who likes to scribble in margins, cross things off with a bold pen, or needs space to sketch (and re-sketch) your plans, I've got something just for you.

Grab the free companion Sketch Planning Workbook!

DOWNLOAD IT NOW AT

followmyarrow.com/sketchworkbook

It's packed with:

- Printable and digital-friendly time block templates
- Reflection prompts to keep it real
- Tools to help you define your Kings (aka your must-dos)
- Space to plan, adjust, and celebrate your progress

Whether you're a pen-and-paper planner or a digital sketcher, this **free** workbook will help you bring everything in this book to life—your way, on your terms.

Because let's be honest: we moms plan better when we've got the right tools—and a little space to think.

Dedication

To every mom who bought the color-coded planner, the fancy stickers, and the dream that this would finally be the year you got it all together—only to find out the book fair is today, not next week, and your kid's supposed to be dressed like a character from a *Dr. Seuss* book but showed up in her school uniform.

This book is for you.

You are not failing. You are not forgetful. You are not lazy. You're just working with a life that changes course about twelve times a day and didn't come with a pause button or an assistant.

Sketch Planning isn't about squeezing more into your already-packed day. It's about freeing yourself from the mental load, ditching the guilt, and finding a rhythm that flexes with your life. Like yoga pants for your brain.

Let's do this.

Preface

Let me guess... you've tried a million planners.

Digital ones. Paper ones. Color-coded, spiral-bound, sticker-covered ones that promised to "simplify your life" but somehow made it more complicated.

Me too.

I bought them all.

I followed the systems.

I time-blocked until I wanted to throw my planner out the window.

But no matter how much I color-coded or tried to squeeze my day into perfect little boxes, I kept feeling the same way: overwhelmed, behind, and like I was doing it wrong.

That's the thing no one tells you—most planning systems are built for a version of life that doesn't include curveballs, caregiving, mental load, or kids who suddenly remember they need a costume for school... tomorrow.

What I needed wasn't more structure.

It was more flexibility.

More grace.

More space to be human.

So I created Sketch Planning.

It's not about doing more. It's about doing what matters, without losing your mind—or your momentum.

This book isn't here to fix you.

Because you're not broken.

You're busy. You're brilliant. You're building a life in real time, with real responsibilities and real interruptions.

And you deserve a planning system that gets that.

What you'll find in these pages isn't perfection. It's peace.

It's tools that bend instead of break.

It's rhythms instead of rigid rules.

It's practical, simple, and totally okay to scribble on.

Whether you're running a business, raising babies, or both at once—this is for you.

Because your time matters.

Your peace matters.

And your plan should reflect *your* life—not someone else's highlight reel.

So grab a highlighter (if that brings you joy), a crayon (if that's what's available), or just your brain and a Post-it—and let's sketch a life that actually works for *you*.

You ready?

Let's go.

CONTENTS

Introduction

Raise your hand if you've ever started your day thinking, *"I've got this,"* only to end it wondering how your entire plan fell apart by 10 a.m.

That was me—more times than I care to count. I used to believe I was just "bad" at time management. I'd look at other women with neat planners and perfectly packed lunches and think, *What do they know that I don't?* So I bought the sticker planners. I blocked every hour. I even color-coded my tasks and added motivational quotes in the margins. Spoiler alert: none of it stopped life from happening.

Like the time I found out—*at drop-off*—that it was "free dress" day (A.K.A. wear what you want, no uniform day). My daughter had asked me if I was *positive* it wasn't something special that day (she reminds me frequently that she doesn't trust me lol). In that moment I had a very strong clue that I'd forgotten to check the calendar... again. That reminder had been written down, but not in a time block. Just sitting there quietly on the page, like it expected me to remember on my own. Ha.

Or how about this one: I had a whole day lined up—meetings, content deadlines, errands, the works. And then, bam! Surprise early release at school. Or my personal favorite: I woke up sick (like, the kind of sick that makes your bones ache), and still had a full day staring at me from my planner like, *"Hope you're ready!"*

But here's the thing: once I started using Sketch Planning, days like that didn't feel like failure anymore.

With this method, I had a system that *flexed* with me. I could rework the day without mentally spiraling. If a meeting ran long, I knew exactly what tasks I could shift. If school let out early or I had to take a sick day, I could move everything around without starting from scratch or losing my mind. Sketch Planning gave me the freedom to say, *"This didn't go as planned... but I've got this."*

That's why I created this system—and why I'm sharing it with you.

Sketch Planning is not a rigid method designed to turn your life into a spreadsheet. It's a flexible, visual approach that helps you figure out what truly matters each day, and gives you the mental space to breathe when life throws spaghetti at your schedule.

In this book, we're going to walk through the three main pieces of the system:

Kings – Your non-negotiables. These are the big rocks of your day—the things that absolutely have to happen.

Easily Moved Tasks – Your flexible friends. These are important but can shift around without everything collapsing.

Time Blocks – Your structured pockets of time. Not every minute of the day, just the realistic chunks that help you stay focused.

And yes, I'm bringing stories—because if I've juggled work, school drop-offs, unexpected puke-fests, and client calls while cooking mac and cheese, chances are... you have too.

This book isn't just a guide—it's a lifeline. One that helps you go from *"What even IS today?"* to *"Okay, let's adjust and keep going."*

Let's ditch the guilt, toss the rigidity, and build a rhythm that works *with* your life, not against it.

1

Introduction to Sketch Planning

Understanding the Limitations of Traditional Planning

Let's talk about planners for a minute.

You know the ones—the kind with tabs for every month, layouts for every week, and an entire page just for stickers that say things like "You got this!" and "You did a thing! Go you." I used to love those planners. I'd spend a ridiculous amount of time decorating them. The stickers were adorable, and filling in each little box gave me a false sense of productivity. I'd sit down with my iced decaf caramel macchiato, ready to conquer the week like I was starring in my own productivity YouTube video.

But here's the thing no one tells you: by the time you finish stickering your way through the page, there's no room left to actually write anything important—like "Dress like your favorite book character day" or "Library books due."

Even when I *did* remember to write those things down, I wasn't blocking out time for them. They were just sitting there, floating in the white space of my planner, hoping I'd somehow *remember* to act on them amidst the chaos of the day. I didn't.

And don't get me started on rigid time blocking. According to the planners, I'm supposed to fit everything neatly into hour-long boxes. But life doesn't work in boxes—it works in "somewhere-between-picking-up-the-kid-and-feeding-the-dog" blobs. Sure, maybe something fits in a 3–4 hour window, but the odds of it happening at *exactly* 10:30 a.m.? About as likely as my dog not barking during a Zoom call.

Here's what actually happens:

It's a typical Tuesday. I've done the school drop-off, tossed in a load of laundry, grabbed my iced coffee (priorities), and sat down to handle emails. I've got a nice little to-do list. I've even carved out a block for writing… but suddenly, I try to update something and end up resetting my password 7 times and I can't find my charger… again. I was *just* using it..

Or I wake up feeling like I got run over by a toddler-sized flu truck. My whole day gets thrown off. With a traditional planner, I'd spiral. Cue the stress, the guilt, and the inevitable feeling that I've already failed before lunch.

That's the problem: traditional planning systems don't account for the realities of *real life*. They assume your day will go as planned. That your energy will be consistent. That your kids won't randomly need a purple shirt and matching socks for Spirit Week.

They also assume you'll feel okay about rewriting your entire day when things shift—which, let's be honest, just leads to more overwhelm.

Here's the truth: I'm not bad at planning. And neither are you. We're just living in a world that doesn't fit neatly into stickered squares and color-coded time slots.

That's why I created Sketch Planning. Because moms (and really, anyone with a life) need a system that bends with them. We need something that says, *"Hey, it's okay if your plan changes. We can shift. We can move things. We can still win the day, even if it looks different than you thought it would."*

And if all else fails? Quote a movie, grab another iced macchiato (or whiskey), and laugh about it later with your husband while your kids stare at you like you're speaking another language. (Because honestly, quoting *Tommy Boy* is sometimes all that gets us through.)

Sketch Planning isn't about being perfect. It's about giving yourself the freedom to *be a person*—a gloriously messy, quietly organized hot mess of a person who actually gets things done. Even when life doesn't go according to plan.

Introducing the Sketch Planning Method

Okay, so we've agreed that traditional planners are basically the equivalent of a pair of jeans from your early 20s: cute in theory, deeply uncomfortable in practice, and clearly not made for your current life. Now let's talk about what *does* work—something I call **Sketch Planning**.

This method is my not-so-secret weapon. It's simple. It's visual. It's flexible. And most importantly, it respects the reality that your day might look one way at 8 a.m. and completely different by 2:30. (Especially if someone forgot their gym shoes.)

With Sketch Planning, your day becomes a canvas instead of a rigid grid. Think of it like doodling out your day—strategically. It works on paper, a whiteboard, your favorite note-taking app, or the back of your kid's math homework in a pinch (been there). The tools don't matter. The method does.

Here's the breakdown:

1. Kings (The Non-Negotiables)

These are the biggies. The must-dos. The *if-this-doesn't-happen-we're-in-trouble* items. They're your pillars for the day.

Examples?

- A client Zoom call you can't reschedule
- Your daughter's orthodontist appointment
- School pickup (unless you enjoy getting passive-aggressive office calls)

These things are not flexible. You plan the rest of your day *around* them.

Once, I had three meetings lined up and a blog post due. And then—curveball—my daughter had a half-day. My *actual* planner was like, "Well, good luck with that." Sketch Planning was like, "No problem. Your meeting is a King, and so is school pickup. Everything else can move."

2. Easily Moved Tasks (The Shuffleable Stuff)

This is your supporting cast. They're important, but they can be rescheduled, bumped to tomorrow, or done in that weird 30-minute gap between dropping off dry cleaning and reheating your lunch.

Things like:

- Replying to emails
- Filing receipts
- Watering the plants
- Writing the thank-you note you meant to send three weeks ago (no judgment)

I love this category because it gives you breathing room. These tasks don't demand perfection—they just need a place to land.

3. Time Blocks (The Spacious Anchors)

Unlike traditional time blocking that insists "you must write your proposal from 10:00 to 11:00 on the dot," Sketch Planning time blocks are *flexible*. Think of them like wide, cozy windows where things can happen *within* a general period.

I like to block out 3–4 hour chunks. For example:

- Morning Work Block (8:30–11:30ish): Answer emails, tackle 1–2 priority tasks
- Afternoon Block (1:00–4:00): Client meetings, errands, editing
- Evening Block (7:00–9:00): Quick work check-in, then family time

This allows for real-life things—like spontaneous Target runs, spilled juice, or long-winded kids recounting every detail of their school day ("And THEN we walked to lunch…").

You're not married to the clock here—you're just giving yourself dedicated zones of time to get stuff done, without feeling like a failure if it doesn't start at exactly 1:03 p.m.

How It All Works Together

Here's where the magic happens:

- Start with your **Kings**. Put them down first so you don't double-book or forget something huge (like being a parent).
- Add your **Time Blocks**. These give your day structure without locking you in a planner prison.
- Fill in your **Easily Moved** tasks wherever there's space—or wherever they make sense energy-wise.

It's basically the "realistic mom version" of planning. It knows you might not feel like doing spreadsheets at 9 a.m., and that sometimes dinner becomes "whatever we can microwave in under 4 minutes."

And the best part? When life goes sideways (because it will), you're not ripping pages out of a planner or mentally berating yourself. You're adjusting. Shifting. Reworking without the panic.

Because Sketch Planning doesn't demand perfection—it gives you permission to pivot.

The Benefits of Sketch Planning

A.K.A. How to plan your life without crying into your coffee.

So now that you know what Sketch Planning is, let's talk about why it's worth trading in your sticker-heavy, time-block-obsessed, spiral-bound stress trap.

First off, Sketch Planning is like brain decluttering—but without the pressure to suddenly become Marie Kondo. It pulls everything swirling in your head (appointments, tasks, random mental reminders like "buy dog food" or "Google weird rash on kid's leg") and gets it out where you can see it. And bonus: you don't need a color-coding system that requires a legend.

It clears your mental clutter

You know that feeling when you open your planner and immediately feel like you're failing because *nothing* is going according to schedule? Been there. More than once.

Sketch Planning says, "Hey, no worries. Let's move a few things around."

It takes the pressure off. Instead of staring at a to-do list so long it looks like a CVS receipt, you get a clear, visual layout of your *real* priorities—what must get done and what can wait without the world ending.

It reduces stress (like, a lot)

Picture this: You're sick. Not like a "little sniffle" sick, but a "why-do-my-eye-balls-hurt" kind of sick. Old planner you would stare at your day thinking, *I'm behind, I'm failing, I can't do this.*

Sketch Planning You? Says, *"Let's slide these Easily Moved tasks to tomorrow, keep that one King task, and build in a nap block."*

Instead of spiraling, you're adjusting—and still getting the most important things done. It feels like magic. Or like finally drinking your iced coffee while it's still cold.

It gives you flexibility *and* momentum

Let's be real: time-blocking sounds productive until your 10 a.m. "deep work" slot gets derailed by a dentist call, a sick kid, or your dog doing something suspicious in the next room.

Sketch Planning thrives in the unpredictable. You plan with intention, but also with the understanding that life doesn't run on a timer. By building your day around blocks—not strict hours—you can still feel accomplished, even if nothing happened *exactly* when you thought it would.

It's permission to be productive without being perfect.

It works for families, too

This system isn't just for solo use. I've used it with my entire family to avoid the "*Wait, you didn't tell me there was a concert tonight*" conversations. (Which are always followed by someone looking confused while wearing mismatched socks.)

You can create shared visual plans that show the Kings for each family member—like doctor's appointments, soccer practice, or that one random school spirit day you almost forgot. (Looking at you, Pajama Day.)

When everyone can *see* what's happening, it cuts down on chaos. And the passive-aggressive sighs. Win-win.

It helps you stay focused without burning out

Sketch Planning encourages you to work with your energy, not against it. You're not forcing yourself into unrealistic schedules—you're giving yourself tools to prioritize what really matters and make space for the rest.

And when you do finish a Time Block or knock out a King? You feel like a rock star. Like the kind of mom who remembers the library books *and* dinner.

(Not gonna lie, I still sometimes forget the library books. But at least now I know where to move that task and how to bounce back without beating myself up.)

Bottom line? Sketch Planning is the gentle, adaptable system that actually works with your real life—not the imaginary one you wish you had on Pinterest.

You don't need more pressure to perform.

You need a plan that gives you grace, space, and a bit of wiggle room for when your kids crack you up, your dog eats your sticky notes, or you're a few chips you stole while making your kids lunches becomes your breakfast.

Next up? I'll walk you through **Setting Up Your Sketch Planner**, so you can make this method your own—whether you love paper, apps, sticky notes, or scribbling on napkins.

Ready to make your own flexible planning space? Let's do it.

Setting Up Your Sketch Planner

So, you're ready to set up your Sketch Planner—which, I promise, is not code for "make a vision board that would make Martha Stewart weep." This is where the *real-life magic* begins, and I'll walk you through everything.

Remember, the goal here isn't to create something beautiful (although you *can*)—it's to create something *useful*. Your setup should fit your life, your brain, and your season—whether that season is "thriving businesswoman" or "hiding in the pantry for five minutes of silence."

1: Choose Your Planning Style (Your Vibe = Your Flow)

Let's find your ideal setup style based on how you naturally think, plan, and function. There's no one right way, only *your* right way.

Paper & Sticky Notes Galore (Low-Tech but High-Impact)

This method is for you if:

- You like seeing your plan laid out physically

- You enjoy crossing things off (hello, dopamine)
- You tend to forget things if they're hidden in an app

Use:

- A sheet of paper or journal
- Sticky notes in different colors
- A big desk calendar or wall chart if you like the "command center" vibe

Bonus: You don't run out of those adorable stickers like you do in traditional planners. (Seriously, I always use the pretty ones by March. Then what? Just motivational quotes and regret.)

Digital Tools for the Tech-Savvy Mom Boss

This one's for you if:

- You live on your laptop or phone
- You like things clean, color-coded, and synced
- You want flexibility and drag-and-drop ease

Great tools:

- Trello (my favorite for visual cards)
- Notion (flexible and super customizable)
- Google Sheets/Docs or Calendar
- Milanote or Miro for a more creative, whiteboard-style layout

Pro Tip:

Create three columns: **Kings**, **Easily Moved**, and **Time Blocks**. Then drag tasks around as needed throughout your day or week.

This is great if you travel, bounce between kids' practices and errands, or work online and need your plan to go wherever you do.

Whiteboard Warriors & Visual Thinkers

You're a visual thinker if:

- You need to *see* the big picture
- You're a tactile person who likes writing, wiping, and redoing
- You want your plan visible to the whole family

Use:

- A whiteboard divided into 3 sections
- Magnetic notes or washable markers
- Color-coding per family member or type of task

Family Tip:

Add school events, work meetings, and your husband's "surprise plans" (AKA forgetting to tell you he invited people over). That way everyone can see what's happening—and maybe stop asking you 27 times a day what's for dinner. (Maybe.)

2: Pick Your Rhythm (Daily? Weekly? "Survival Mode"?)

Sketch Planning is beautifully adaptable. You don't have to plan every day the same way. Here are a few rhythms you can try:

The Morning Quick Sketch

Start the day by mapping out what's ahead, adjusting for any new curveballs, and choosing your top priorities. Do this with coffee in one hand and low expectations in the other.

Perfect for:

- Moms who like a quiet moment before the chaos
- People who wake up with no idea what day it is (*raises hand*)

Evening Wind-Down Reset

This is my favorite. After dinner, once the girls are showering or winding down, I sit with my bourbon on ice and jot down the basics for tomorrow.

What are my Kings?

What got bumped today?

Do I need to rearrange my time blocks for anything new?

It feels good to go to bed knowing I've got a handle on what's coming—without locking myself into a rigid schedule that's going to blow up the moment someone gets a mystery rash or a last-minute spelling test.

Weekly Sketch Map (Sunday Brain Dump Edition)

This is great for visualizing your full week ahead. You can roughly sketch the whole week with:

- Known events (Kings)
- Ideal work or chore time blocks
- Flexible to-dos scattered in

Optional: Light a candle, grab snacks, wear comfy socks. This should *not* feel like corporate planning. You're not running a boardroom—you're managing a household, a business, and your sanity.

3: Customize It (This Is *Your* Sketch Plan)

Make it your own. Use your favorite pens. Make doodles in the margins. Add movie quotes if it makes you smile.

Your plan should reflect *your life*—not some influencer's curated desk space. If you prefer scribbles and arrows to polished layouts? That's valid. If your plan lives in five places (whiteboard, paper, phone, fridge)? That's fine too.

My truth bomb:

Most days, I still feel like a hot mess. But when I look back at my Sketch Plan and realize I did the big things—showed up for my work, fed my family, moved things forward—I realize I'm way more organized than I give myself credit for.

Sketch Planning doesn't *look* like perfection. It *feels* like peace.

Reminder:

This is your setup. You get to change it. Evolve it. Scrap it and start over if you need to.

Just promise me you won't abandon it because it's not "Pinterest pretty." You're not here to impress anyone. You're here to create a rhythm that *actually works*—even when life doesn't.

How to Identify Your Kings, Easily Moved Tasks, and Time Blocks

where we make Sketch Planning *really* work for you. This system isn't just about writing stuff down—it's about **knowing what belongs where** so you don't end up trying to vacuum during your only work Zoom or realize too late that the recorder was *required today.*

Let's break down the three core pieces of the Sketch Planning method, complete with real-life mom-life context.

1. Kings (The Non-Negotiables)

Your Kings are the things that absolutely have to happen. Like, there's no "I'll get to it later." These are the pillars that everything else in your day balances around.

Think:

- Scheduled work calls or meetings
- School drop-offs and pickups
- Doctor's appointments
- Getting the kid to gymnastics… *in the right leotard this time*

Kings are time-bound or have real consequences if forgotten. You can't shuffle them around (unless you enjoy apologizing to your boss or explaining to the school office *why* your child missed the field trip).

One of my Kings might be a scheduled podcast recording or Zoom call I can't reschedule. Or a school event that I *really* want to remember this time—like Book Character Day, because my daughter is still mildly scarred from the time she went in normal clothes surrounded by kids dressed like The Lorax and Thing 1 & 2.

Tip: Limit yourself to 2-3 Kings a day max. More than that, and you're setting yourself up for stress or disappointment. This is about clarity, not cramming.

2. Easily Moved Tasks (The Flexible Friends)

These are the things that need to get done, but *not necessarily today* and *definitely not at a specific time.* You can shuffle them around like puzzle pieces to make the rest of your day work.

Think:

- Responding to emails
- Creating social media content
- Folding laundry (or at least re-fluffing it for the 3rd time in the dryer)
- Researching summer camps, meal planning, reordering vitamins

If Kings are your high-priority "yes, today" tasks, Easily Moved tasks are your "soon, but not urgent" to-dos. They can be bumped when life gets lifey.

Writing email content for my business is important, but if I have to move it because my daughter volunteered *me* for something at school, it's not the end of the world. It shifts to the next Time Block that makes sense—or the next day entirely. The key is not losing it, just relocating it.

Tip: Keep these on a separate list or color so they don't sneakily take over your entire day. Just because you *could* do them doesn't mean you *should* do them right now.

3. Time Blocks (Your Spacious Planning Zones)

Time Blocks are the structure that holds your day together. But unlike traditional planners that give you 8:00, 8:30, 9:00—and then expect your toddler to cooperate—Sketch Planning says "Let's give this a range."

I like to use 3–4 hour blocks, depending on my day. For example:

Example of My Ideal Time Blocks:

- **Morning Block (8:30–11:30)**: Emails, admin tasks, maybe a meeting

- **Afternoon Block (1:00–4:00)**: Content creation, calls, errands
- **Evening Block (7:00–9:00)**: Quick work catch-up, family time, sketch out tomorrow's plan

Notice how flexible that is? If something runs long, I still have wiggle room. If I need to rearrange the day, the whole plan doesn't fall apart—I just move things between blocks.

Tip: Think of Time Blocks as containers—not cages. You're making room for what matters, not packing every second.

Putting It All Together: A Real-Life Day

Here's a sample Sketch Plan for a Tuesday that goes slightly off the rails:

Before the chaos:

Kings:

- School drop-off7:30
- Client call at 10:00
- School pick-up at 3:00

Easily Moved Tasks:

- Write blog post
- Fold laundry
- Schedule dentist appointments

Time Blocks:

- Morning Block (8:30–11:30)
- Afternoon Block (1:00–4:00)

- Evening Block (7:00–9:00)

You sit down feeling confident.

Then... life.

The client call runs 40 minutes over. Your kid's coach sends a text: "Practice today!" Laundry is still wet. Dinner? TBD.

But instead of panicking, you: Keep your Kings

Shift the blog post to the evening

Bump laundry and dentist calls to tomorrow

Reframe your afternoon block around school pickup and a Target run

You still got your priorities done. You didn't melt down. And your plan flexed with you—not against you.

At first, you'll probably want to overthink where to place things. You might try to sneak in too many Kings. You'll wonder if reworking blocks means you're failing.

You're not. You're adjusting like a total boss.

Sketch Planning is about rhythm, not rigidity.

Grace, not guilt.

And finding your flow in a life that doesn't sit still for long.

2

Mastering the Art of Prioritization: Identifying Your "Kings"

Defining Your Kings

Let's talk about your **Kings**—the real MVPs of your Sketch Plan. These are the things that absolutely *must* happen in your day. Not the "would be nice" stuff or the "if I have time" fluff. Nope. These are the *non-negotiables*.

If your day was a castle (stick with me), your Kings would be the load-bearing walls. You mess with them, the whole thing wobbles—or completely collapses and you're left wondering why your daughter showed up in her school uniform on spring picture day (because Spring pictures call for Sunday best smh).

What Counts as a King?

A King is a task or commitment that:

- Has a set time or firm deadline

- Carries real consequences if forgotten or skipped
- Supports your top priorities (family, health, work, sanity)
- Impacts others if it doesn't get done

This includes:

- Doctor's appointments
- Work meetings or client calls
- School pickups and drop-offs
- Medication or therapy sessions
- Time-sensitive home responsibilities (like taking out trash before garbage day... or remembering it's garbage day at all)

My daughter's school pickup is a King. Every. Single. Day. There's zero wiggle room on that one unless I want to field an awkward call from the school secretary while speed-racing through traffic. Been there. Not a fan.

What's *Not* a King?

Just because something *feels* important doesn't mean it's a King. (This part can be tricky, especially for us overachievers.)

Not Kings:

- Organizing the spice cabinet
- Rewriting your Instagram bio
- Shopping for throw pillows (even if they're on sale and you *really* want to refresh the living room vibe)

- Deep cleaning the fridge *unless something is actively oozing*

Those might be important later—or emotionally satisfying (looking at you, beautiful clear container and labeled pantry)—but they don't go in the King category.

Why Defining Kings Matters

When you start your plan with too many non-negotiables, your day gets top-heavy and overwhelming fast. That's when the stress hits. That's when you say things like, "I have so much to do but I have no idea where to start," and then wander into the kitchen and forget what you're doing.

But when you *clearly identify your 2–3 real Kings* for the day? Suddenly things click. You know where to focus your energy. You know what has to happen, even if your schedule gets sideswiped.

You can't do everything, but you can always do your Kings. That's success.

How to Spot Your Real Kings

If you're unsure whether something is truly a King, ask:

- Will something fall apart if I don't do this today?
- Is someone depending on me to follow through?
- Does this support my core values (family, health, work, mental peace)?
- Will this create a domino effect if ignored?

If yes to any of these? It's a King.

If no? Slide it into the Easily Moved category or bump it to later in the week.

Common Traps (and How to Avoid Them)

Trap #1: Everything Feels Like a King

That's not your schedule talking—that's your *stress brain*. When everything feels urgent, nothing really is. Take a breath and re-evaluate. If the world won't end and nobody's calling you about it? It's probably not a King.

Trap #2: Guilt Kings

These are tasks you feel like you *should* do, but they're not actually urgent or required. For example, hosting a perfect playdate or baking homemade muffins for the PTA. Lovely? Sure. Essential? Not today, friend.

Trap #3: Invisible Kings

These are the things you always do without thinking—school pickup, medication, logging into work—and sometimes forget to plan for because they're just "automatic." But when you don't account for them, your day feels packed before it even starts.

The Power of Getting Your Kings Right

When you define your Kings first, you set your day up for success. You give yourself:

- **Clarity:** You know exactly where to start.
- **Confidence:** You're not wondering if you forgot something important.
- **Control:** Even if everything else gets bumped, the critical stuff gets done.

At the end of the day, when your brain is fried and the dog still hasn't been walked, you can still say, *"I did what mattered today."*

And that, my friend, is the whole point.

Prioritizing Your Kings

So now you've identified your Kings—yay! You've got your non-negotiables front and center and you know what *must* happen today.

But what happens when your list of Kings is longer than you'd like (hello, back-to-back appointments, birthday cupcakes, AND a dentist visit)? Or when all your Kings are crammed into the same two-hour window like they didn't get the memo to space themselves out?

That's where **King prioritization** comes in.

Because even among your must-dos... some are a little more "royal" than others.

Why Prioritizing Your Kings Matters

When you know which Kings carry the most weight, you can:

- Stay calm when your day goes sideways
- Make confident decisions about what to tackle first
- Avoid that overwhelmed "Where do I even start?" spiral
- Free up mental space to actually *do* the thing instead of just thinking about it

Strategy 1: Rank by Impact

Ask yourself:

If I only got ONE thing done today, which King would have the biggest impact?

That's your true #1.

Think in terms of:

- Deadlines: Which King is time-sensitive?
- Consequences: Which one will create the most chaos if skipped?
- Energy return: Which task, once done, will make the rest of your day smoother?

If I've got three Kings—school pickup, client Zoom call, and prepping dinner—school pickup wins. Not because I *want* to do it more, but because forgetting it would throw the whole house into panic mode.

Once I lock that in, I can plan around it.

Strategy 2: Match Kings to Your Energy Windows

We all have different peak energy times. Maybe you're a morning unicorn who can get things done at 6:30 a.m., or maybe you hit your groove after dinner. Either way, try to match your most demanding King to your highest-functioning block.

Ask:

- When do I think most clearly?
- When do I feel most focused?
- When am I least likely to be interrupted by snack requests or group texts?

My brain works best mid-morning, after I've dropped off my daughter, started laundry, fed the dog, and answered a few emails. That's when I tackle "deep work" Kings—like recording content or writing. I save simpler Kings (like scheduling a call or reviewing copy) for the afternoon when I'm a little more brain-fried.

Strategy 3: Stack Kings + Block Accordingly

If you have multiple Kings, group them into blocks where they naturally fit. Example:

- **Morning Block:** Bookkeeping + email follow-up
- **Afternoon Block:** School pickup + errands
- **Evening Block:** Prep for tomorrow's launch

This lets you *see* the flow of your day and prevents King traffic jams. No more piling three heavy tasks into the same hour and wondering why you're stressed before lunch.

Strategy 4: Know When to Reassign a "King"

Sometimes what *feels* like a King… turns out to be a pushy little imposter. Ask:

- Can I delegate this?
- Can I reschedule it without real consequences?
- Is this more of a guilt task than a true King?

Confession:

I've definitely treated things like "bake cupcakes from scratch" as Kings—until I realized I could *buy* them, and my daughter would still think I was a rockstar. Prioritize sanity over perfection every time.

Strategy 5: Use the 3-King Rule (It's Not Just Catchy, It's Critical)

To avoid overwhelm, limit yourself to **3 Kings per day**.

Why 3?

- Because life happens
- Because your brain and schedule need space

- Because it forces you to choose what truly matters

Anything beyond 3? Treat it as a *bonus King* or bump it to tomorrow. Trust me—you'll feel so much more capable and less chaotic when your list doesn't demand the impossible.

Bonus: Weekly King Mapping

Some Kings aren't daily—they're weekly. A quick weekly overview can help you:

- Spot overload days before they hit
- Spread Kings more evenly
- Avoid bottlenecks like "everything's due Thursday!"

You can use a sticky-note board, digital planner, or a simple grid to map your week's top 2–3 Kings per day.

I do this Sunday night, whiskey in hand, while my kids debate what show to rewatch for the 100th time. It's a five-minute reset that makes a huge difference.

Sketch Planning is all about grace and flexibility. Even your Kings can move *if absolutely necessary.* Prioritizing helps you stay focused—but if life throws a wrench in your plan, you adjust like the flexible queen you are.

Remember: You don't have to do *everything.*

You just have to do *what matters most today.*

Scheduling Your Kings

Alright—so you've named your Kings. You've lovingly created Time Blocks that flex with your life. Now it's time to *marry the two* in a way that won't have you pulling your hair out by lunchtime.

Because knowing what your Kings are is half the battle. The other half? Actually putting them *into* your day where they'll get done—and not crushed under an avalanche of emails, snacks, and "Mom, where are my socks?"

1: Plug Your Kings in *First*

Think of your Time Blocks like containers. And your Kings? Those are the heavy rocks that go in first.

You've probably heard that old metaphor about filling a jar with rocks, pebbles, and sand—if you put the sand in first, you'll never fit the big stuff. Same deal here.

Your King tasks go in first—before you schedule anything else.

This tells your brain (and your planner) what absolutely needs your time and attention.

If I have a Zoom call at 10 a.m., that goes in my **Morning Block** *before* I even think about dropping in "respond to comments" or "update the Canva template I've been avoiding." Kings lead the day. Everything else follows.

2: Choose the Best Block for Each King

Each King needs a home—and not just *any* time block. You want to match it with:

- The **time it's scheduled for** (duh)
- Your **energy level**
- Your **life logistics** (like school pickup or errands)

If a King is a high-focus task (like writing, creating, presenting), place it in a time block where your brain is at full power. If it's a logistical one (like appointments, school pickup, errands), match it with the most realistic part of your day.

Use this little cheat sheet:

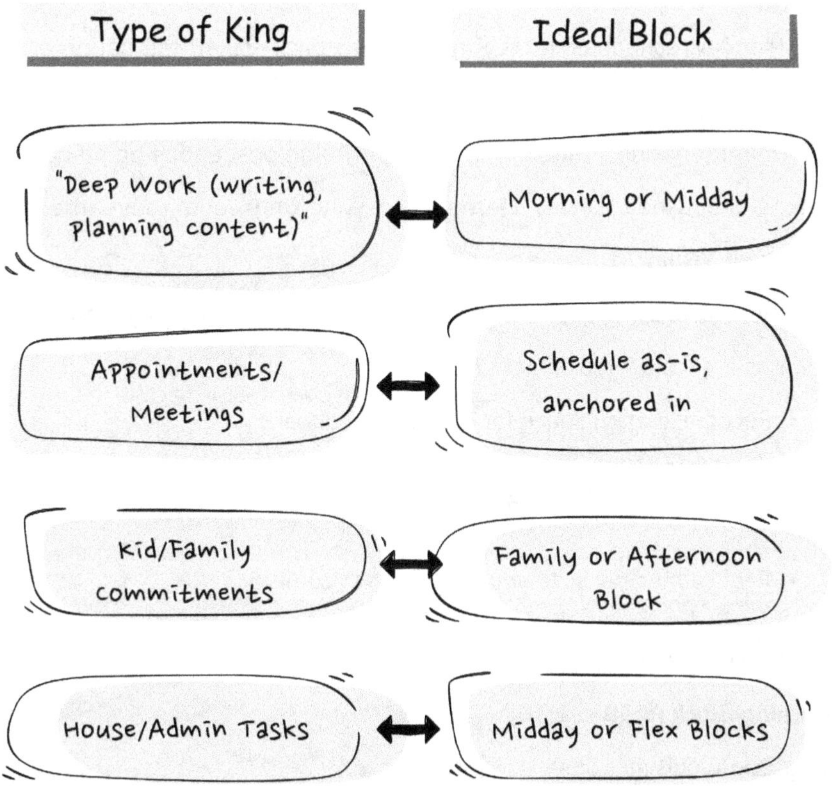

3: Avoid King Clumping

Resist the urge to jam all your Kings into one Time Block unless they naturally flow together. If you stack them too tight, you're setting yourself up to fall behind early—and that's when the spiral starts.

Instead:

- Space them throughout your day
- Buffer at least 15–30 minutes between intense tasks
- Treat school pickup and drop-off as legit commitments (because they are)

One Monday I scheduled three Kings back-to-back—client call, daughter's eye appointment, and a big blog draft. I *thought* I could squeeze them all in. But the appointment ran long, I missed lunch, and my blog post ended up being... let's say, "extra unpolished." Lesson learned: give your Kings room to breathe.

4: Make It Visual

Whether you're using paper, a whiteboard, or an app—physically seeing where your Kings are inside your blocks helps you:

- Recognize open space for Easily Moved tasks
- Avoid accidental overlaps
- Feel calmer, because you know what's coming

Quick visual example:

Morning Block (8:30–11:30)

King: Zoom Call @ 10:00

Easily Moved: Respond to emails

Easily Moved: Reorder groceries

Afternoon Block (1:00–4:00)

King: School pickup @ 3:00

Easily Moved: Review course content

Easily Moved: Vacuum couch again (thanks, dog)

Evening Block (7:00–9:00)

King: Sketch tomorrow's plan

Optional: Finish blog draft if brain allows

5: Adjust Without Guilt

Remember: Sketch Planning is built to flex. If one of your Kings has to move:

- Shift it to another open Time Block
- Trade it with another task
- Delegate if possible
- Reschedule (if it truly can move—check that it's not just Guilt King energy)

There are days I realize halfway through my Morning Block that one King needs to shift. Maybe I didn't sleep well, or the school called (again), or I just need a moment. I've learned to give myself grace. Moving a King isn't failure—it's strategy.

Bonus Tip: Track Your King Wins

At the end of the day, check in:

- Did I complete my Kings?
- If not, what got in the way?
- What do I need to adjust for tomorrow?

Even if your Easily Moved tasks went untouched and the laundry is still in the washer (oops), *if you completed your Kings, you won the day.*

Let yourself feel good about that. Really.

Sketch Planning is not about doing all the things. It's about doing the *right* things—and protecting the space for them in a way that *feels doable.*

Quick Recap

- Kings get scheduled **first**—they're the anchors of your day
- Match them to your energy and availability
- Don't stack too many into one block
- Visual planning helps prevent chaos
- Be ready to adjust (without spiraling)

Handling Unexpected Interruptions to Your Kings

Let's just get this out there: **life will interrupt your plan.**

It's not a matter of *if*, it's a matter of *when*.

That's not a flaw in your system. That's just real life doing what real life does—usually around the same time you sit down

But here's the Sketch Planning difference: **you don't fall apart when the plan does**.

Instead of crumbling under a missed time block or ruined to-do list, you adapt—intentionally, calmly (ish), and with confidence.

First: Pause Before You Panic

When something throws off your plan—take a breath.

Ask yourself:

- *What just happened?*
- *Which King is affected?*
- *Can I still make this work today—or do I need to shift something?*

I once had a Morning Block mapped out perfectly: respond to emails, finish a lead magnet, and hop on a call at 10. Then—ding! School nurse. My daughter got hurt at recess and needed to be picked up.

Old me: stress spiral.

Sketch Planning me: reshuffled the Easily Moved tasks, moved the call back 30 minutes, and tossed the lead magnet to the next block. Did I get it all done? No. Did the world end? Also no.

Reworking Your Kings on the Fly

Here's how to pivot like a planning ninja when something derails a King:

1. Can you move the King to another Time Block today?

If yes—easy fix. Slide it over and adjust the surrounding tasks.

2. Can it be rescheduled for another day?

Some Kings *feel* urgent but can actually wait 24 hours. Check the consequence level. If it's just ego yelling at you, not the calendar—reschedule.

3. Can it be broken into smaller parts?

If a King task feels too big now (because your mental space just got hijacked), break it into mini tasks.

Ex: "Record video" becomes "outline video" "set up camera" "record intro"

4. Can you delegate or outsource it?

Yes, this includes things like asking your spouse to handle school pickup or letting your kid eat cereal for dinner while you finish a time-sensitive task. Delegating isn't failure. It's strategy.

Your Flexibility Formula

Use this quick little checklist to reset in the moment:

What *must* still happen today?

What can move to another block?

What can move to tomorrow (or next week)?

What can I hand off entirely?

What needs to just... not happen (and that's okay)?

If your whole plan fell apart and all you did was your Top 1–2 Kings? Still a win.

I've had days where I've had to completely erase my afternoon block and switch to "survival mode." That looked like reheating leftovers, canceling a meeting, and getting *one* task done. And guess what? That one task was a King. I still counted the day as a win.

Real-Life Interruption Scenarios + Responses

Surprise school pickup needed?

Move your current King to the next block, replace it with a short 5–10 minute task (if you have time), or postpone it. School pickup becomes your new King.

Client meeting runs over?

Move or drop your next King if needed. Move Easily Moved tasks into tomorrow. Order takeout if dinner just became optional.

Sick day? (Yours or the kids')

Switch to a minimal version of your plan. Focus only on one King max. Nap if possible. Forgive everything else.

Technology fails? (Because of course it does)

If you lose access to a digital tool, pivot to paper or voice memos. Kings can be adapted, re-captured, and re-scheduled later.

Emergency Flex Block (Yes, It's a Thing)

Pro Tip: Build in a Flex Block once or twice a week—a catch-all space for:

- Kings that got interrupted
- Overflow from chaotic days
- Buffer time between tasks or just life catch-up

Call it your "In Case of Emergency" block.

Even if you never use it (lol, you will), it gives you peace knowing it's there.

Permission to Let Go

Some days? The interruption *is* the King.

Your child's meltdown, your own mental health crash, the flat tire, the urgent call from your sister—those things matter.

When life pulls rank on your plan, *that doesn't make you undisciplined.*

It makes you a human who's planning like a realist.

And when you respond with *intentional adjustment instead of panic*? You win. Every time.

Planning Doesn't Prevent Interruptions—It Prepares You for Them

Sketch Planning doesn't promise perfection. It promises **resilience**.

And that's what makes it so powerful.

You don't crumble when life does.

You adjust. You shift. You roll with it—and still come out with your priorities (and your sanity) mostly intact.

And hey—if all else fails, pour yourself a shot of whiskey and start again tomorrow.

Reviewing and Adjusting Your Kings

So here's the thing no one tells you about planning: **it's not one-and-done.**

Life shifts. Schedules change. Kids go through phases (so. many. phases). And your priorities evolve right alongside it all.

Which means your Kings—the things you treat as non-negotiables—need to evolve, too.

Sketch Planning isn't about making a rigid list of "forever important" things. It's about **staying honest** about what matters *right now*, and being flexible enough to adjust without guilt.

Why Review Your Kings Regularly?

Let's be real: what *used to be* a King might not need to be one anymore.

Some tasks sneak into King status because of habit, people-pleasing, or panic—*not because they're truly essential.*

By regularly reviewing and adjusting your Kings, you:

- Reclaim time and mental energy
- Stay aligned with your actual values and goals
- Stop doing stuff that no longer makes sense just because "you always have"

For a while, I treated "daily Instagram content" as a King in my business. But when I sat down and reviewed what was actually moving the needle (and what was draining my time and energy), I realized… it wasn't that important. It quietly got demoted to an Easily Moved task. And I haven't looked back.

When to Review Your Kings

You don't need a complicated process or quarterly retreat (unless that sounds fun to you). Just a regular rhythm to pause and reflect.

Here's what works well:

Weekly Review

Every Sunday night (or whenever your week resets), look at the Kings you scheduled:

- Did you complete them?
- Were there too many?
- Did any feel like false urgency?
- Did you actually *need* all of them?

Monthly Reset

Look at the big picture:

- Are the same Kings showing up repeatedly?
- Are they still aligned with your current goals and season?
- Is something new becoming more important?
- Is there a lingering task pretending to be a King out of guilt or fear?

What to Ask Yourself During a King Review

Use these questions to clarify what stays—and what needs to change:

1. **Was this task truly non-negotiable?**
2. Or did I just feel like I *should* do it?
3. **Did completing it move me forward?**
4. In life, work, or peace of mind?
5. **Would I be okay if I didn't do this again next week?**
6. If yes... maybe it's not a King.
7. **Did it drain me more than it helped me?**
8. Sometimes we realize certain tasks come at too high a cost.
9. **Was this someone else's priority—or mine?**
10. Oof. This one stings. But it's important.

Kings Can Change, And That's the Point

What's a King this week might not be next week.

What used to be an afterthought might need to move up the priority ladder now.

Maybe right now:

- Your King is helping your teen with college applications
- Or it's taking a daily walk for your mental health
- Or setting boundaries around work hours so you're more present with your kids

These matter. Even if they're not "productive" in the traditional sense. Especially then.

There have been seasons where I needed to make *rest* a King. Not "rest when everything else is done" (because it never is)—but *true*, scheduled-in, "I will guard this time like a dragon" kind of rest. If that's where you are, that's valid. You don't need to earn your rest with productivity.

How to Adjust Without Overthinking It

Here's your step-by-step:

1. **Delete or downgrade any recurring King that's no longer worth your time.**
2. Move it to Easily Moved or off your list altogether.
3. **Elevate any recurring task that consistently causes chaos when ignored.**
4. Welcome it to the King circle.
5. **Replace filler Kings with value-aligned ones.**
6. If you've been putting "organize junk drawer" in your plan to feel productive, maybe it's time to replace it with "prep content for launch" or "plan quality time with the kids."
7. **Reflect, don't obsess.**
8. This isn't about being hyper-critical. It's about being honest and intentional.

Optional Habit: The King Log

If you're into journaling or tracking (but not in an overwhelming way), try keeping a short list of the Kings you scheduled each day or week.

Over time, you'll see patterns—what keeps showing up, what fades away, what feels good, and what drains you.

And when you look back and realize you've dropped 3 "fake Kings" and replaced them with things that actually *support your life*? That's growth, baby.

Your Kings Should Reflect Who You Are Now

Planning isn't about keeping things the same—it's about helping you change and grow *on purpose*.

So if your Kings shift? Good. That means you're paying attention.

And if you adjust your focus midweek, midmonth, or midmorning because something more important shows up? You're not failing. You're *evolving*.

Let your plan evolve with you. It was always meant to.

3

Embracing Flexibility: Working with 'Easily Moved' Tasks

Identifying Easily Moved Tasks

If Kings are the must-dos—the "drop everything, this matters" kind of tasks—then **Easily Moved Tasks** are your behind-the-scenes support crew. They don't need the spotlight. They're helpful, often important, but very rarely urgent.

They're the tasks that *keep life running*, but also give you wiggle room to adapt, breathe, and *not* crumble when a Time Block gets hijacked by a surprise science project or an emotional teenager decides *this* is the moment to have a deep talk

What Exactly *Is* an Easily Moved Task?

Easily Moved Tasks are:

- **Flexible:** They don't need to happen at a specific time

- **Shiftable:** You can reschedule them without panic or guilt
- **Non-urgent:** They're valuable, but not time-sensitive
- **Batchable or delayable:** They don't create instant chaos if skipped for a day or two

Think of them as the soft edges of your day—the ones that help fill in gaps, provide momentum, and give your Kings room to breathe.

Common Examples of Easily Moved Tasks

Let's break this down with some real-life mom and business-owner examples (ahem, hi):

- Folding laundry (aka fluff cycle #3)
- Replying to non-urgent emails
- Brainstorming future blog post ideas
- Ordering household supplies
- Vacuuming the stairs
- Planning next week's Instagram posts
- Updating your business expense tracker
- Prepping dinner if takeout is an acceptable backup
- Giving the dog a bath (unless it rolled in something terrible—then we're back in King territory)

How to Spot an Easily Moved Task

When you do your brain dump or list your to-dos, ask:

1. **Does this need to happen *today*?** If not Easily Moved.
2. **Can I delay this without negative consequences?** If yes Easily Moved.
3. **Is it attached to a deadline or someone else's timeline?** If no Easily Moved.
4. **Would forgetting it today lead to a guilt spiral or just a minor inconvenience?** If it's more "meh" than meltdown Easily Moved.

Why These Tasks *Still* Matter

Just because these tasks are flexible doesn't mean they're unimportant. They're often:

- The ones that help your future self
- The little things that reduce friction in your routines
- The pieces that keep your home, business, or brain functioning smoothly

But the difference? You don't need to *squeeze them in* at the expense of your energy or peace. You slot them in *when it makes sense.*

How to Use Easily Moved Tasks in Your Plan

1. Create an "Easily Moved" Pool Have a designated space—sticky notes, whiteboard corner, a digital list—where all your Easily Moved tasks live until you assign them to a Time Block.

2. Match Tasks to Energy + Open Space Feeling focused but don't have any Kings at the moment? Grab an admin task. Low energy but want to check something off? Do a quick 5-minute to-do. Found an open 30 minutes because your meeting got canceled? Pull one from your pool.

3. Don't Overpack Your Blocks A good rule of thumb: 1–3 Easily Moved tasks per Time Block (max).

More than that = overwhelm in disguise.

My truth:

I used to treat my "flex time" like a dumping ground. I'd try to cram in seven tasks because "they're not *that* big." I always ended up behind and discouraged. Now? I cap myself at 2–3 max per block. It's realistic—and way more satisfying when I actually get them done.

Warning: When Easily Moved Tasks Pretend to Be Kings

It happens.

Tasks sneak in under the radar, *looking* urgent but really just wearing a stressy disguise.

For example:

- Organizing your inbox because you're procrastinating something bigger
- Deep cleaning the pantry on a Wednesday at noon because Instagram made you feel behind
- Rewriting your blog post for the third time instead of hitting publish

Check yourself: Is this actually urgent... or am I avoiding something else?

Easily Moved = Mental Margin

Here's why this category is so powerful:

It gives you the *margin* to live.

When a Time Block gets hijacked, you shift these without guilt.

When you have extra energy or a rare quiet house, you tackle them and feel awesome.

They allow you to feel **productive without pressure**.

You don't *have* to do them today... but when you do, they're like bonus points for your sanity.

Not All To-Dos Deserve King Status

Letting go of the idea that everything must be urgent is *liberating*.

Easily Moved tasks remind you that not everything is make-or-break.

And when you build a plan that includes both your highest priorities *and* your flexible ones—you create a rhythm that works *with* your life, not against it.

You get structure, freedom, and space to breathe.

And isn't that the point?

Prioritizing Easily Moved Tasks

Easily Moved Tasks are awesome—until they multiply like rabbits and start crowding your plan with "oh yeah, I meant to do that" energy. The trick? Knowing which ones are worth your time *today*... and which ones can chill a little longer.

Because flexibility without intentionality = chaos.

But flexibility + purpose = power.

Why Prioritize Your Easily Moved Tasks?

Not every flexible task deserves your energy right now.

If you try to tackle them all at once, you'll burn out—or get distracted trying to reorganize your pantry *again* instead of sending that invoice.

Prioritizing these tasks helps you:

- Avoid low-value time traps
- Make the most of your energy and availability
- Stay focused on the *right* "nice-to-dos" instead of the *urgent-but-not-actually-important* ones

The Sketch Planning Filter: Urgency vs. Importance

Let's break it down:

Urgent + Important = DO SOON

These are sneaky tasks that aren't full Kings, but still matter soon.

Examples:

- Finalizing a grocery order for delivery tomorrow
- Responding to a non-crisis but time-sensitive client email
- Buying a birthday gift before the party this weekend

These are the Easily Moved tasks you **do today** or plug into your *next available* block.

Important But Not Urgent = PLAN IT

These are meaningful—but not on fire.

Examples:

- Writing next month's blog post
- Organizing digital files for smoother workdays
- Updating your long-term budget

These deserve attention, but can be scheduled for later in the week, in a focused block.

Urgent But Not Important = DELEGATE, AUTOMATE, OR BUMP

This is "false urgency" stuff. It feels pressing… but if you didn't do it, nothing major would happen.

Examples:

- Replying instantly to every message
- Re-sharing someone else's post right this second
- Rerouting Amazon returns when the deadline isn't close

These either get:

- Delegated (yes, your kids *can* help return library books)
- Batched later
- Delayed until it actually matters

Neither Urgent Nor Important = IGNORE FOR NOW

This is the clutter that sneaks into your day when you're tired, bored, or trying to feel productive.

Examples:

- Re-color coding your calendar
- Researching yet another meal planning app
- Cleaning your baseboards (unless they're *actually* growing things)

Let them go. Or file them in a "Someday When I'm Bored" list (spoiler: that list never gets touched—and that's okay).

The Easily Moved Task Filter in Action

Example from my real day:

Brain dump:

- Refill prescription
- Fold laundry
- Send Pinterest pins to VA
- Order birthday balloons
- Reschedule dentist
- Research travel options
- Clean the fridge

Now run the filter:

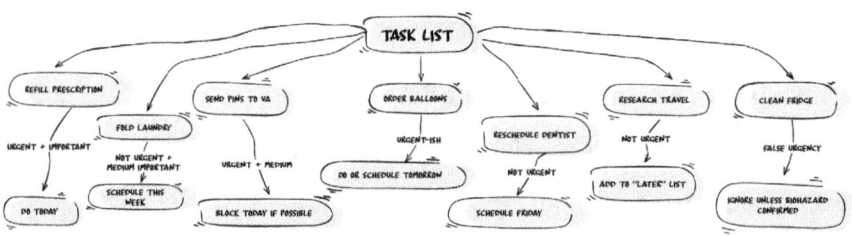

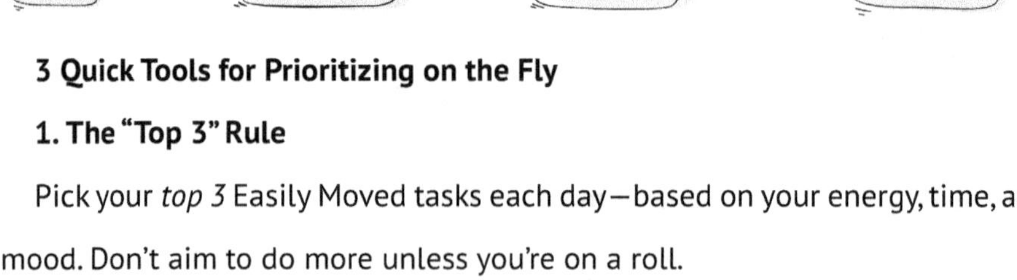

3 Quick Tools for Prioritizing on the Fly

1. The "Top 3" Rule

Pick your *top 3* Easily Moved tasks each day—based on your energy, time, and mood. Don't aim to do more unless you're on a roll.

2. The "15-Minute Task" Shortcut

Got a short block of time? Keep a list of tasks that take under 15 minutes. Knock out one between meetings or during a lull. *Quick wins = major mental relief.*

3. The "Good Enough" Option

Ask: What's the simplest version of this task that gets it done?

Examples:

- Can't meal prep for the week? Just write a quick dinner list.
- Don't want to clean the whole house? Wipe down the counters and move on.
- Too tired to update your entire Pinterest strategy? Just pin five things today.

Progress > Perfection. Always.

Bonus: Stack Low-Energy Tasks at the End of the Day

Your brain doesn't want to make decisions at 7 p.m.

So put your lowest-stakes Easily Moved tasks at the end of your Evening Block. That way, if you skip them? No guilt. If you do them? Victory dance.

My Tip:

Sometimes I leave "fold laundry" or "reorder vitamins" in the Evening Block—not because I *will* do them, but because it's nice to have the option *if* I feel like being a responsible adult after dinner.

Flexible ≠ Forgettable

Just because a task is Easily Moved doesn't mean it should be eternally postponed.

When you take 5 minutes to prioritize these little guys? You reduce stress, keep your life humming, and *actually feel on top of things* (even when you're in your mom bun and pajama pants at 2 p.m.).

This is where the Sketch Planning system shines:

You're not overloading your day—you're *intentionally shaping it.*

Scheduling Easily Moved Tasks

Let's be real—uninterrupted, gloriously focused time is basically a myth for most of us. What we *do* have? Weird 15-minute windows between appointments, surprise gaps in our day, and that magical hour where no one is yelling and the house is... quiet-ish.

This is where **Easily Moved Tasks** shine.

They're like puzzle pieces—you can pop them into your schedule wherever they fit. And when used well, they help you stay productive *without overloading* your brain or your Time Blocks.

Why Schedule Them at All?

Easily Moved Tasks are flexible—but that doesn't mean they should be forgotten.

If you don't assign them a place, they'll pile up, hang out on your mental checklist, and whisper guilt at you while you're trying to enjoy your evening show. (We've all heard that whisper. It's rude.)

Scheduling them intentionally:

- Keeps your to-do list from becoming a monster

- Creates natural flow and progress throughout your week
- Helps you feel like "hey, I'm actually on top of life right now" (a rare but glorious feeling)

1: Find the Gaps in Your Time Blocks

Every Time Block should have *some* breathing room built in—not packed wall-to-wall with Kings.

Look for:

- Extra time in blocks with only one major task
- Buffers between appointments or school pickups
- Post-lunch lulls or evening downtimes
- Canceled meetings

My real life example:

After I finish a King in the Morning Block, I often have 20–30 minutes of "what now?" energy. That's the perfect moment to knock out a small Easily Moved task—something like reordering printer ink or updating a resource list. It's quick, satisfying, and doesn't fry my brain.

2: Pre-select 1–3 Easily Moved Tasks Per Day

You don't need to schedule *all* of them.

That's how we fall into the "crammed planner = crushed soul" trap.

Instead, each morning (or the night before), look at your list and choose 1–3 to focus on for that day.

Pick based on:

- How much time you *actually* have

- Your energy level
- What would feel satisfying to finish

Bonus Tip: Add one "easy win" to your list—something you know you can knock out quickly. It builds momentum and makes you feel like a capable human before lunch.

3: Use Rolling Placement

Here's a simple trick that keeps your Easily Moved tasks fluid—but not forgotten:

- Create a "This Week" list (on paper, a sticky note, or in a digital tool)
- Drop your prioritized tasks into Time Blocks as your day unfolds
- At the end of the day, move anything undone to the next available block
- No guilt, no mess, no erasing required

This rolling structure means no Easily Moved task gets left behind (unless it deserves to be).

My Tip:

I use a sticky note column on my whiteboard titled "Still To Place." As I plan my day, I grab a few from that list. The rest stay visible but non-urgent. It's like a buffet of low-pressure productivity.

4: Match Task Type to Time Type

Not all tasks are created equal—and neither are the little time pockets in your day. Match them up for maximum efficiency.

Time Available	Best Task Type
10 - 15 Minutes	Quick admin (emails, online orders, updates)
30 Minutes	Light focus tasks(review something, schedule calls)
45 - 60 Minutes	creative or thinking tasks (write, edit, batch work)
Low-energy	chores, auto-pilot admin, phone calls
High-energy	writing, strategizing, anything you've been avoiding

5: Don't Overschedule—Stack for Success

Even if your list of Easily Moved Tasks is 12 items long, do *not* schedule all 12 in a single day unless you want to cry by dinner.

Instead:

- Group similar tasks together in one Time Block (email batching, errand running, admin)
- Stack them *after* your Kings—not before
- Treat finishing *any* of them as a win

- Leave space for life to happen (because it will)

Bonus: The "Back Pocket" Task List

Keep a tiny list of 3–5 micro-tasks you can do when your day goes off the rails. These are the tasks you don't *plan* to do, but that feel good to accomplish if you find yourself with a surprise block of time.

Examples:

- Clean out one inbox folder
- Update your email signature
- Jot down 3 blog post ideas
- Restock the bathroom with toilet paper
- Cancel that subscription you forgot about

These tiny wins add up fast—and they give you a sense of control on days that feel bananas.

Little Tasks Deserve Strategy, Too

Just because you *can* move a task doesn't mean it should float around aimlessly forever.

Sketch Planning helps you create a flow that feels smart, doable, and flexible enough for real life—with all its interruptions, half-drunk coffees, and last-minute school emails.

By choosing the right time for your Easily Moved tasks, you make space for forward motion without the burnout.

Let's be clear: **just because a task is "easily moved" doesn't mean it's yours forever**.

Easily Moved Tasks are often the ones we carry out of habit—laundry, errands, refilling the soap dispenser, responding to non-urgent messages—because we think, *"It's faster if I just do it."*

And sometimes, it is.

But often? It's not.

Or at least, it's not *worth* being the default person forever.

That's where delegation comes in.

Why Delegation Belongs in Sketch Planning

Sketch Planning isn't about doing more—it's about doing what *matters* most.

Which means you need time and energy for your **Kings**.

Delegating Easily Moved Tasks:

- Frees up your schedule and brainpower
- Helps others up (yes, even the kids!)
- Keeps your blocks clear for the stuff *only you* can do
- Reduces the build-up of low-level stress and micro-decisions

My truth:

I used to think I had to do it all—because I could. But just because I can change the lightbulbs, schedule the vet appointment, and buy the birthday gift doesn't mean I should. Delegating just a *few* of these things made my days feel *so* much lighter.

What to Delegate? Start With These

The best candidates are tasks that:

- Don't require your unique brain or creative touch
- Have clear instructions or outcomes
- Pop up frequently and suck your time in tiny doses
- Can be passed off without guilt (or with only mild guilt we'll work on later)

Great Easily Moved Tasks to Delegate:

- Reordering groceries
- Running returns
- Scheduling appointments
- Household chores (laundry, dishes, vacuuming)
- Picking up or mailing items
- Checking voicemails or sorting mail
- Posting or pinning pre-written content
- Entering data or uploading files

Who Can You Delegate To?

- **Your partner** – **Pro Tip:** be specific. "Handle dinner" = vague. "Pick up pizza on the way home" = success.
- **Your kids** – Yes, they can put away laundry, unload the dishwasher, return library books, and set the table (even if it's not perfect).

- **Your team or VA** – If you run a business, start handing off those digital tasks like formatting, uploading, scheduling posts, or creating graphics from templates.

- **Apps or automations** – Not a person, but still valid! Set reminders, subscribe to auto-ship, or use tools like HoneyBook, Trello, or ClickUp to streamline your workflow.

One of the best things I did in my business was give my VA a recurring list of Easily Moved Tasks. Instead of constantly asking "Can you do this?", I created a shared doc she pulls from anytime she has extra time. Game changer.

Step-by-Step: How to Delegate Without Losing Your Mind

1. Choose 1–3 tasks to test

Start small. Don't hand off your whole life in one day. Pick a few clear, low-stakes tasks and see how it feels.

2. Clarify the outcome (not just the process)

Instead of saying *"Do it like this,"* say *"Here's the end result I need."*

Let people find their own way to get there. (*Yes, even if they don't fold towels your way.* Deep breaths.)

3. Create a recurring delegation list

Keep a running list of tasks you *can* and *should* delegate. It makes it easier to hand things off quickly when your week gets busy.

4. Follow up with encouragement, not micromanagement

If you find yourself redoing someone else's version of the task, pause. Ask: *Was it really wrong, or just different from how I would do it?* (Oof, I know.)

5. Celebrate the mental load you just removed

Seriously. Even if someone else loaded the dishwasher weird. You didn't have to do it. That's a win.

When Delegation Becomes a Sketch Planning Habit

As you build this muscle, you'll start asking:

- *"Do I need to do this myself?"*
- *"Who else could own this?"*
- *"What would free me up for a higher-value task—or even a break?"*

When your default answer is no longer "I'll just handle it," you'll have space for:

- More energy for your Kings
- Less resentment at the end of the day
- A team (at home or work) that feels trusted and capable
- Actual room to breathe

You're Still in Charge—You're Just Not Doing It All

Delegating isn't giving up control.

It's choosing to lead your home, work, and life like a CEO—not a burned-out middle manager doing *all the things* because she thinks she has to.

And in Sketch Planning, that's exactly what we're aiming for:

Simplicity, flexibility, and the freedom to focus on what matters most.

Eliminating Unnecessary Easily Moved Tasks

It's okay to admit that not everything on your list is worth your energy.

Not today. Not tomorrow. Possibly… *ever.*

We've all been guilty of carrying tasks from one week to the next like we're emotionally attached. And why? Because they seem *useful* or *productive*—but in reality, they're clutter.

Easily Moved Tasks should serve you, not drain you.

And if they're no longer serving you?

It's time to show them the door (nicely, but firmly).

Why This Matters

You only have so much:

- Time
- Energy
- Brainpower
- Patience for tasks that feel like they matter but actually… don't

So if you're spending any of those precious resources on things that don't move the needle, lighten your load, or improve your life? That's a hard no.

Letting go of these time-wasters isn't lazy.

It's efficient. Strategic. Empowered.

And honestly? It feels amazing.

1: Audit Your Easily Moved Task List

Once a week (I like Sunday nights with my low ball), scan through your running list of Easily Moved Tasks and ask:

- **Have I carried this task from one week to the next more than twice?**
- **What would actually happen if I didn't do this?**
- **Is this something I *want* to do—or just feel obligated to?**
- **Is this meaningful, or just noise?**

You'll be surprised how many "do I really need to do this?" moments pop up.

2: Identify the Task Clutter

Here's what might need to go:

Outdated To-Dos

That "follow up on class party list" reminder? The party happened three weeks ago. Byeee.

Busywork Disguised as Productivity

You don't need to update your Pinterest board covers *again*. You don't need to alphabetize your spice drawer every month.

(Unless you love doing it. In that case, do it with joy. But if it's a "should" task, release it.)

Tasks Based on Other People's Expectations

Like that project you said yes to because you felt guilty... but it makes you dread opening your inbox.

Or the "be more active in that Facebook group" note that's been haunting your list for six months. If it's not aligned with your actual goals or values? Let it go.

Self-Imposed Perfectionism

You can send the email without redesigning the entire header.

You can post the blog without rewriting the conclusion for the fifth time.

I once had "refresh website footer" on my Easily Moved list for three months. Every week I bumped it forward. Why? Because I thought it mattered. It didn't. I deleted it. The footer survived. I'm still alive. All is well.

3: Clean House (Without Guilt)

Delete, archive, cross out, or stick a "not worth it" emoji next to the tasks you're done babysitting.

Your time is too valuable for:

- Guilt tasks
- Repetitive rethinking
- Low-impact effort
- Endless "maybe someday" clutter

Try this mantra:

"If it doesn't serve my priorities, protect my peace, or spark momentum—it's out."

4: Prevent New Clutter from Sneaking In

Now that you've cleared the junk, keep it that way by asking yourself this *before* you add something new to your Easily Moved list:

- *Is this truly important?*
- *Can I commit to doing this in the next 7 days?*
- *Would future me be grateful—or overwhelmed—by this task?*

If it's not a yes... it doesn't go on the list.

Keep a separate "maybe someday" parking lot if you're not quite ready to let it go—but don't let it clog your daily flow.

Bonus: Enjoy the Space

Now that you've trimmed the fluff?

You'll be amazed at how much lighter your day feels.

You might find yourself:

- Finishing blocks early
- Actually resting during breaks
- Getting to the "fun" stuff you usually put off
- Or—dare I say—doing nothing and not feeling bad about it

My Tip:

After my first real Easily Moved purge, I had space to take a guilt-free walk after dinner instead of trying to knock out "one more thing." I came back feeling like a whole new person. It really is the little things.

You Don't Owe Every Task Your Energy

You are allowed to stop doing things that no longer make sense.

Cutting the excess isn't slacking—it's streamlining.

It's editing your day with intention.

And it's creating space for the *right* things, not just *more* things.

Let your Easily Moved list work *for* you—not against you.

4

Structuring Your Day: Mastering 'Time Block

Defining Time Blocks: Creating Structured Segments in Your Day

If Kings are your priorities and Easily Moved Tasks are your flexible fillers, **Time Blocks are the rhythm that holds it all together.**

They're the scaffolding of your day—the structure without the suffocation.

Because we're not about hourly micromanaging here. That's what sent you running from traditional planners in the first place, right?

Time Blocks give you *enough* structure to stay focused, but not so much that you crumble when someone gets a fever, the dog eats a sock, or the Wi-Fi goes out mid-Zoom.

What *Is* a Time Block, Exactly?

A **Time Block** is a flexible 2–4 hour chunk of your day that you dedicate to a *type* of work or activity—not a specific task at a specific minute.

It's not about cramming in 12 things or writing "10:15–10:45: fold socks."

It's about creating space for focused intention—knowing *what* you're doing in each stretch of time without micromanaging *how.*

Think of it as a container, not a cage.

Why Time Blocks Work (Especially for Moms)

- They match the real, unpredictable rhythm of mom life
- They keep you focused without boxing you into the minute-by-minute
- They help your brain batch energy and decision-making
- They give you permission to *not* be productive all the time
- They make adjusting on the fly *so* much easier

I used to try planning my day in strict 30-minute slots. It looked great—until life happened. A spilled drink, a school call, a client reschedule... and the whole plan unraveled. Time Blocks saved me from starting over 10 times a day. Now I just shift the block—or what's in it—and keep going.

How to Create Your Time Blocks

Start with what you already know about your day. Use natural breaks or patterns as a guide—like school drop-off/pickup, meals, energy levels, or work windows.

Here's a basic formula to get you started:

Example Time Blocks (Adjust to Fit Your Life):

Block Name	Time Range	Focus Area
Morning Block	8:30 - 11:30	Focus work, admin, deep thinking
Midday Block	12:00 - 3:00	Errands, meetings, home chores
Afternoon Block	3:30 - 6:00	School pickup, kids activities, prep
Evening Blocks	7:00 - 9:00	Wind-down, light work, planning

If you're up early, you can add a **Wake-up Block (6:00–8:00)** for your quiet time, workouts, or getting kids ready.

If you're a night owl, consider a **Late Night Block** for creative bursts or solo downtime.

Give Your Blocks Purpose

Instead of saying "I'll do this task at 10:45," you say, "This task fits in my Morning Block."

That one shift? It changes everything. You:

- Reduce stress when something takes longer than planned
- Stop beating yourself up for being "off-schedule"
- Start thinking in *flows*, not rigid appointments

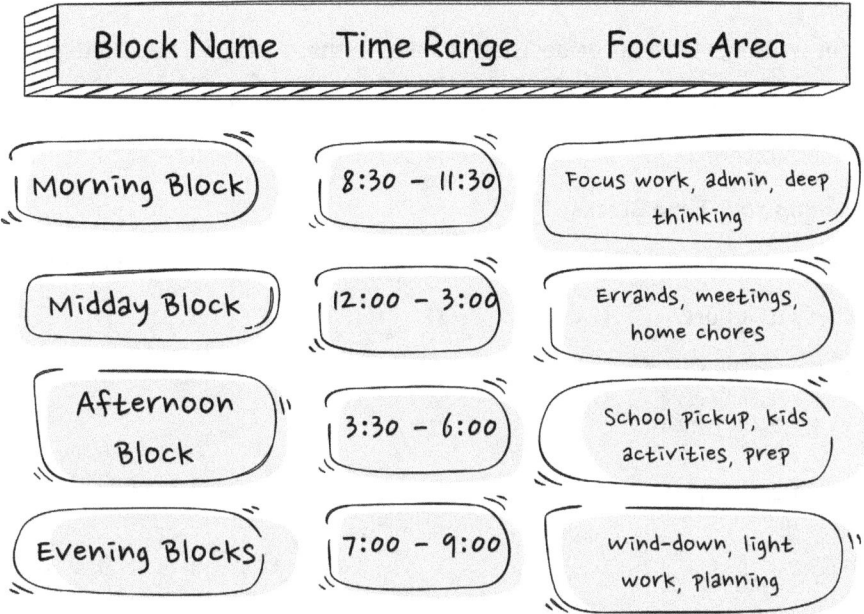

My Morning Block is my go-to for anything that requires brainpower. I know if I put writing, planning, or decision-making in that window, I'll actually get it done. My Afternoon Block? That's for errands, pickups, and stuff I can do with half a brain cell.

Naming Your Time Blocks

Give them names that *feel* good—not just "Block 1," "Block 2." That's boring and easy to ignore.

Try names like:

- Focus + Flow
- Power Block
- Catch-Up Zone
- Rest + Reset
- Admin Sweep
- Creative Core
- Family Hour

You don't need to rename them every week—but giving them personality makes them easier to connect with. It turns your plan into something you *want* to look at.

Time Blocks Don't Have to Be Filled

Just because a block exists doesn't mean it needs to be stuffed with to-dos.

You can have:

- A Rest Block

- A Free Space Block
- A "Let's See What Happens" Block
- A Family Fun Block (yes, it counts!)

Planning isn't about doing more.

It's about doing *what matters* and giving it the space it deserves.

Time Blocks Create Your Day's Rhythm

They help you shift from reactive to proactive.

From scattered to intentional.

From stressed to, "Oh look, I *planned* to have room for this surprise."

By defining your Time Blocks, you set yourself up for calm, control, and a day that works for *you*—even when life doesn't go according to plan.

Allocating Time Blocks

If we're not intentional, our days fill up with demands—and it's no surprise we feel burned out by the time we finally sit down.

Time Blocking isn't just about productivity. It's about *balance*.

You're not just building a daily schedule—you're building a *life you can actually enjoy living in*.

So let's talk about how to allocate your Time Blocks in a way that serves your priorities *and* protects your peace.

Why Balance Matters in Your Time Blocks

Because you're not just a mom.

Or just a business owner.

Or just the household manager/chef/errand-runner-in-chief.

You're a whole human.

And whole humans need:

- Time to work
- Time to rest
- Time to breathe
- Time to exist without being needed every second

If your blocks are all filled with output and none with input? Burnout is coming for you with snacks and a megaphone.

I used to think "rest" had to be earned. That if I didn't check off enough, I hadn't "earned" downtime. But Sketch Planning taught me that rest isn't a reward—it's fuel. If I want to show up for my Kings tomorrow, I have to recharge today.

1: Identify Your Key Categories

Every person's blocks will look different, but generally they'll fall into these areas:

Typical Time Block Categories:

- **Work/Business**: focused tasks, calls, admin
- **Household**: errands, laundry, cleaning
- **Family**: school runs, meals, activities, homework
- **Rest/Recharge**: naps, quiet time, scrolling TikTok guilt-free

- **Personal**: reading, hobbies, workouts, journaling
- **Prep/Planning**: setting up the next day, grocery list, meal prep

Now the trick is giving each category the *space it deserves*—without stacking everything into back-to-back, energy-draining blocks.

2: Allocate Based on Your Life (Not a Pinterest Ideal)

Sketch Planning is not about building an aesthetic schedule—it's about building a *functional rhythm* that actually works in your season of life.

Start with anchors:

- What time do your kids get up and go to school?
- When do you need to do pickup, meals, appointments?
- What time do you feel *on* vs. *meh*?

Then, fit your block types around that.

Example from My average weekday:

Block Name	Time	Category	Notes
Morning Focus	8:30 - 11:30	Work	content, creative tasks, meetings
Midday Flex	12:00 - 2:30	Household /admin	Errands, laundry emails
Afternoon Family	3:00 - 5:00	Family	Pickup, snack, homework zone
Evening Reset	6:30 - 9:00	Rest + Planning	Dinner, family time, sketch plan

It's not perfect. But it *flows*—and that's what we're after.

3: Protect Your Rest + Personal Blocks

This is where most women need a loving nudge.

Your **Rest** and **Personal** blocks are *not optional extras.*

They're not "maybe, if I have time" tasks.

They are *part of the plan.*

Without these, your schedule might look successful, but *feel* exhausting.

Ideas for restful blocks:

- Reading with a hot drink
- Listening to a podcast in the car *alone*
- A bath, a walk, or just scrolling aimlessly in peace
- A phone call with someone who fills your cup

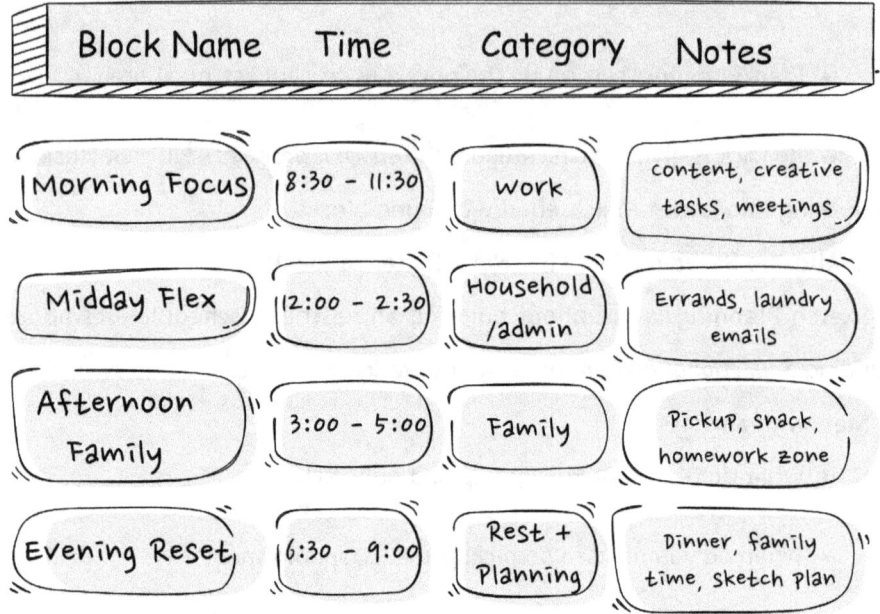

I used to skip my evening "wind-down" block thinking I was being efficient. Nope. I was just setting myself up to crash later in the week. Now I sketch plan my next day while watching a show with my family or sipping whiskey, and it's *so much better.*

4: Mix and Match—Don't Overload

Try not to put two high-effort blocks back-to-back (like deep work deep cleaning).

Instead, alternate focused and lighter blocks.

For example:

- **Morning** = Work
- **Midday** = Errands/admin
- **Afternoon** = Family
- **Evening** = Recharge

If your whole day is "go go go," your energy will hit a wall.

If you're intentional with your Time Block flow, you'll still have energy *at the end of the day*—which is kind of the dream, right?

Bonus: Weekly Time Block Themes

Once you've got your daily flow down, you can take it a further by lightly theming your weeks.

For example:

- **Monday:** Admin + Planning
- **Tuesday:** Creative work
- **Wednesday:** Errands + Flex Tasks

- **Thursday:** Calls or content batching
- **Friday:** Family/fun/light catch-up

This makes assigning tasks to blocks even easier—and keeps your brain from decision fatigue every morning.

Balance Isn't a Perfect Split—It's a Felt Sense

Your goal isn't to equally divide every block between work, rest, family, and fun.

Your goal is to *feel like you're living a life that works for you*—not one that's happening to you.

And when you allocate your Time Blocks with that in mind?

You'll find more ease, more energy, and (let's be honest) fewer 9 p.m. meltdowns.

Optimizing Time Blocks

You've got your Time Blocks mapped out.

You know what's happening when.

Now you want to make those hours count—*without feeling like a machine.*

Because the goal here isn't hustle for hustle's sake.

The goal is **intentional energy use**—working smarter inside your blocks so you get more done *and* protect your sanity.

Let's make your Time Blocks work for you, not just exist on paper.

Why Optimization Beats Overloading

Time Blocks give you structure. But if you fill them with too many tasks, vague ideas, or distractions, they'll still leave you feeling scattered by the end of the day.

Optimizing a block means:

- Knowing what matters most in that block
- Setting up your space and brain to focus
- Keeping distractions at bay (looking at you, fridge and phone)
- Leaving margin to *breathe*

Think of it as curating your block—not just throwing everything into it like a junk drawer.

1: Define the Goal of the Block

Before a block starts, ask:

"What do I want to walk away from this block having done?"

It might be:

- "Write 1 email and batch 5 pins"
- "Catch up on household laundry"
- "Do two admin tasks and prep dinner"
- "Rest without checking my email" (yes, *that* can be a goal)

Clarity = focus.

If your block has 17 competing goals, your brain will bail before you even begin.

I keep a sticky note on my desk with the current block's top 1–3 tasks. It keeps me grounded when I catch myself spiraling into "ooh I should reorganize my files" mode.

2: Start with a Block Ritual

This doesn't have to be fancy. Just something simple that tells your brain: *"Hey, we're shifting into focus mode now."*

Examples:

- Light a candle
- Set a timer
- Open a specific playlist
- Close all other tabs (including that shopping cart you keep forgetting to empty)
- Take three deep breaths

Your brain thrives on cues. Build a little "block starting ritual," and your mind will start showing up *ready.*

3: Use the Power of Time Chunks

Within each Time Block, break your work into mini chunks.

This is where the **Pomodoro Method** or **45/15 rule** can come in clutch:

- 25–45 minutes focused work
- 5–15 minute stretch, snack, or reset
- Repeat once or twice
- Then *stop* and transition to the next block

This works with your natural attention span—and prevents you from burning out halfway through the block.

If I've got a 3-hour Morning Block, I'll usually do two deep-focus chunks of 45 minutes each, with short breaks in between. Then the last 30-ish minutes is for quick tasks or overflow.

4: Eliminate the Sneaky Time Thieves

You know the ones:

- That "quick email check"
- Notifications pinging during a task
- The tab you open "just to grab a link" and then suddenly you're on Etsy
- Tidying up instead of doing the thing you *planned* to do

Build a distraction-free bubble as best you can:

Silence notifications

Use "Do Not Disturb" mode or apps like [Forest, Focus Keeper, Freedom]

Keep a notepad nearby to offload "oh shoot I forgot" thoughts

Set boundaries with your environment (aka: warn your family with a "mama's in her focus bubble" sign if needed)

5: Batch Tasks by Type

Trying to switch from writing to cleaning to calling to editing all in one block = brain whiplash.

Instead, use each block for one general type of energy:

- **Creative/Thinking:** writing, planning, decision-making
- **Admin/Execution:** emails, forms, uploads, logistics

- **Movement/Errands:** housework, groceries, school stuff
- **Rest/Recovery:** napping, journaling, scrolling with zero guilt

When your brain stays in the same lane, you get into flow faster—and stay there longer.

6: Give Yourself a Soft Ending

Instead of slamming into the next block or task, wrap up each Time Block with:

- A 2-minute review: *"Did I do what I intended?"*
- A quick brain dump if something needs to move to another block
- A check-in: *"Do I need a break before the next thing?"*

This mini reset helps your brain shift gears more smoothly, so you don't carry stress or momentum from one block into the next.

Your Time Blocks = Your Superpower

When you optimize your Time Blocks, you're not just "getting things done."

You're creating a rhythm that supports your brain, your energy, and your goals.

You're staying focused where it matters.

You're giving yourself breaks on purpose.

You're getting more done—with *less* chaos.

And most importantly? You're making your time feel like it actually *belongs* to you again.

Adapting Time Blocks

We've all had those days:

You planned it. You blocked it. You even color-coded it.

And then life said, "LOL, no."

Your kid wakes up with a fever.

Your client reschedules last minute.

You suddenly remember you volunteered to bring cupcakes... today.

Cue panic?

Nope. Not anymore.

With Sketch Planning, these disruptions don't destroy your day—they just trigger a shift.

Because the magic of Time Blocks isn't in the plan itself.

It's in your ability to *adapt* the plan without unraveling.

Real Talk: Life Is Built to Interrupt You

And honestly? That's not a bug in the system—it's the system.

The goal isn't to build a rigid day that falls apart with the slightest detour.

The goal is to build *resilient rhythms* that can bend without breaking.

Flexibility is a strength—not a sign that you're "bad at planning."

So when your Time Blocks get interrupted (and they *will*), here's how to stay grounded and responsive instead of frazzled and defeated.

1: Pause + Reassess in Real Time

Take 60 seconds. Breathe. And ask yourself:

- What just shifted?
- Which Time Block is affected?

- What was in that block?
- What's the *one thing* that still needs to happen?

Then ditch, delegate, or delay the rest.

One morning, my plan was solid: write a promo email, schedule a webinar, and prep lunch. But as the morning unfolded, the vibe shifted. Energy dipped, focus wandered, and suddenly, the block wasn't flowing like I'd hoped.

So, I grabbed my iced coffee (obviously), took two minutes to reassess, and gave myself permission to pivot. The promo email? Moved to tomorrow. Webinar setup? Also tomorrow. Lunch? Frozen pizza to the rescue.

And you know what? Everything still got done. Just not all today. No meltdown. No failure. Just a small shift—and a big reminder that flexible planning works.

2: Rearrange Like a Puzzle, Not a Failure

When your block gets hijacked, resist the urge to throw out the whole plan.

Instead, *re-block.*

That might look like:

- Compressing two smaller blocks into one
- Swapping today's tasks into a less-full block tomorrow
- Cancelling a non-essential block (and *letting it go*)
- Pushing low-priority items into your "Easily Moved" queue

Think of your day like a puzzle—not a line of dominoes. One shifted piece doesn't ruin everything. It just means a little rearranging.

3: Use a "Flex Block" as Your Safety Net

One of the most powerful things you can do?

Build a Flex Block into your week on purpose.

This is an open window (1–3 hours) where you don't schedule *anything*. It's your insurance policy.

Use it when:

- Tasks get bumped due to emergencies
- You need catch-up time
- You just need to breathe and *not do a dang thing*

My system:

I usually reserve Friday afternoons as my Flex Block. If the week went sideways, I have a place to finish what matters. If everything went smoothly (rare but delightful), I use it for planning ahead—or just chilling. Either way, I win.

4: Reevaluate Your Kings (Gently)

When plans fall apart, ask yourself:

"Do these Kings still need to be today's top priorities?"

Sometimes the answer is yes.

Other times? Not really.

Maybe what was once urgent... isn't.

Maybe your energy has shifted and something else needs your focus.

Maybe your *real* King today is taking a nap so you can parent or work without turning into a snapping turtle.

This isn't lazy. It's leadership. You're leading your day with wisdom, not just a to-do list.

5: Create a "Bare Minimum" Plan for Rough Days

Every mom (and human) needs a backup plan for chaotic days.

This is your **Bare Minimum Block Plan**—what you do when things fall apart but you still want to feel functional.

Example:

- 1 King task (top priority only)
- 1 Easy admin task or chore
- 1 Small win to keep momentum (like folding laundry or sending 1 email)
- Everything else = paused, punted, or parked

If you hit those three things? You win the day.

What *Not* to Do When Your Time Blocks Get Derailed

Here's your friendly reminder of what to avoid when plans change:

Don't try to "catch up" everything immediately

Don't stack your next Time Block with double the to-dos

Don't berate yourself for being "off track"

Don't assume the day is ruined by one interruption

You're not behind—you're *recalibrating.*

Bonus: Track What Worked (and What Didn't)

When the dust settles, take a minute to reflect:

- What helped you bounce back?
- What task could've been bumped sooner?
- Was your day *too* full to begin with?
- Do you need a recurring Flex Block or backup plan?

You're not just planning. You're *learning* what works for your real life.

Sketch Planning evolves with you—and the better you get at adjusting, the less you'll fear disruptions.

Interrupted ≠ Unsuccessful

You're not meant to plan your day to *control* it.

You're meant to plan your day so you can *respond to it* with confidence.

You don't need to restart.

You don't need a new system.

You just need a moment... a shift... and a reminder that you're still in control—even when things change.

And that, my friend, is true flexibility.

The kind that lets you be productive, present, and peaceful—even when life gets messy.

Reviewing and Refining Time Blocks

Time Blocks are like your favorite pair of jeans.

At first, they feel stiff, a little awkward, maybe a bit too snug in places.

But once you break them in, adjust for fit, and maybe roll the cuffs a bit—they start feeling *just right*.

Your schedule deserves that kind of customization, too.

So once you've used your Time Blocks for a week or two (or even a few days), it's time to check in:

Are they actually working?

Do they fit your *real* life—or just the life you hoped you'd have?

Let's review, refine, and make your blocks even better.

Why Reviewing Your Time Blocks Is Essential

You wouldn't set your GPS once and never course-correct.

Your life shifts. Your energy changes. Your kids grow. Your business evolves.

So your Time Blocks? They need regular check-ins.

Reviewing helps you:

- Spot where things are too tight or too loose
- Eliminate unnecessary stress points
- Notice patterns you wouldn't see in the moment
- Create a more natural, satisfying rhythm for your days

And most importantly—it makes sure your plan is serving *you,* not the other way around.

1: Pick a Weekly Review Time

Just like you'd sketch out your Kings and upcoming priorities, schedule a short 10–15 minute weekly "Time Block Check-In."

When to do it:

- Sunday evening with your shot of whiskey
- Monday morning before you dive into your first block
- Friday afternoon during your Flex Block wrap-up

Whenever you do it, make it *quick, casual,* and helpful.

2: Ask Yourself These Questions

Here's your simple Time Block Review Checklist:

1. **What worked really well this week?**
2. (Ex: "Morning Blocks felt focused. I loved having an Evening Planning Block.")
3. **What felt rushed, stressful, or constantly interrupted?**
4. (Ex: "I'm trying to do too much in my Midday Block.")
5. **Which blocks were underused or neglected?**
6. (Ex: "I skipped Rest Blocks three days in a row.")
7. **Did I plan around my energy—or ignore it?**
8. (Ex: "I put deep focus tasks in the afternoon and flopped hard.")
9. **Did I have enough margin?**
10. (Ex: "No Flex Block meant I ended the week behind and cranky.")
11. **What do I want to adjust for next week?**
12. (Ex: "Move admin tasks to early afternoon when I can still focus but don't want to be creative.")

Jot it down. Highlight what stood out. This doesn't have to be fancy—it just has to be *honest.*

3: Refine Like a Pro (Small Shifts = Big Wins)

You don't need to overhaul everything. Most of the time, one or two small shifts is enough to make your days flow better.

Ways to tweak your blocks:

- Adjust the *length* (too long = draggy, too short = frantic)
- Rename a block so it feels more aligned with its purpose
- Shift focus: turn an "admin" block into a "catch-up + chill" block
- Insert a mid-block break or energy reset
- Build in margin between big blocks (especially family/work transitions)

My tweak:

I used to stack my Midday Block with way too many "Easily Moved" tasks. It looked good on paper... but in real life? It overwhelmed me. Now I split it into two micro-blocks—one for errands, one for admin—and I feel so much more in control.

4: Keep a "Block Log" (Optional but Powerful)

If you're someone who likes tracking patterns, try keeping a **Block Log** for a week or two.

Jot down:

- Which blocks you used
- What you completed
- What felt too heavy/light
- Any "aha" moments

This gives you hard proof of what's working—and what needs adjusting.

You can even color-code or emoji-tag blocks if you're visual.

5: Remember—This Is an Evolution

You are not locked into one version of your Time Blocks forever.

Life will shift.

Kids' schedules will change.

Your energy will fluctuate with the seasons, your hormones, your mood.

And your planning system? It's *designed* to flex with you.

Let go of the idea that a "perfect" block setup exists. Instead, aim for *good enough to function, great enough to feel right.*

A Little Review Creates a Lot of Flow

You don't need to overhaul your system every week.

But a few thoughtful tweaks? They make your blocks feel smoother, calmer, *and* more effective.

This is how you stop "starting over" every month—and instead, keep building a system that grows with you.

Sketch Planning isn't rigid. It's responsive.

And refining your Time Blocks weekly is how you keep that flexibility working *for* you.

5

MANAGING "HANGING TASKS": TACKLING UNSCHEDULED ITEMS

Identifying Hanging Tasks

You ever finish your day—after folding laundry, feeding tiny humans, answering 27 texts, and handling a meeting—only to lie in bed thinking, "*Ugh.* I still didn't do [insert thing you've remembered 16 times already this week]..."?

That, my friend, is a **hanging task**.

It's that annoying little item that just... lingers. It hasn't made it into your planner, but it keeps tapping you on the shoulder. You never *officially* said you'd do it today, but somehow it's making you feel like you dropped the ball anyway.

Sound familiar?

- You *thought* you'd get to it "after lunch."
- It wasn't urgent enough to be a King, but it wasn't unimportant either.

- You've written it down (somewhere... maybe three times).
- It's now become a regular guest star in your 3 a.m. overthinking playlist.

These are the tasks that *seem small*—but left unchecked, they clutter up your mind, erode your confidence, and make your schedule feel like it's bursting at the seams... even if it's not.

The Emotional Weight of Hanging Tasks

Here's why hanging tasks are low-key *exhausting*:

They create this weird mental loop of *"I should do this"* without any follow-through or closure.

And unlike Kings (which you've protected and planned for), or Easily Moved Tasks (which you've consciously chosen to flex), these ones just *float*.

You don't *fully commit* to them...

...but you also don't *fully ignore* them.

So they hang there—in the invisible mental clutter cloud—costing you:

- Attention
- Energy
- Focus
- And sometimes sleep, let's be real

Confession:

There was a two-month stretch where I "meant" to cancel an old subscription service that was charging me $14.99/month. Every week, I'd glance at my to-do list and think, *"Oh, I'll do that later."* I didn't. It took less than five minutes when I finally did it—but the weight of it for eight weeks? Not worth it.

How Hanging Tasks Creep In (Without You Noticing)

They're usually not dramatic or urgent.

In fact, that's why they're dangerous—they're *forgettable but naggy.*

Some show up as:

- That text you need to reply to (but didn't "have the right words" for earlier)
- That paperwork that's been sitting on the corner of your desk for 12 days
- That gift you meant to order, return you meant to make, or thank-you note you *swear* you'll send

Others disguise themselves as:

- "I'll just remember to do it later"
- "This'll only take a second" (and then you forget again)
- "I'll get to that after I [do 10 other things]"

What they all have in common?

No home. No block. No plan.

And when your plan doesn't *include* them, your brain tries to hold onto them manually—which means more stress and less focus for everything else.

The Impact of Clearing Hanging Tasks

Here's the magic:

Even if you *don't* complete them all right away—*just identifying and placing them* creates instant mental relief.

It's like taking them out of your brain's "worry basket" and dropping them into a real, grounded plan. That act alone turns floating anxiety into clear next steps.

You go from: "I have so much to do and I don't even know where to start."

to

"Oh, this task just needs a 15-minute spot in Wednesday's Midday Block. Cool."

And that shift? That's power. That's peace.

When This Chapter Hits Hard (and Why That's Okay)

If you're reading this thinking, *"Oh no, I have at least 12 hanging tasks right now"*—welcome. You're not behind. You're just about to get *ahead* for the first time in a while.

This is the part of Sketch Planning that turns chaos into calm.

Not by working harder.

But by finally seeing what's been quietly draining you...

...and giving it a place (or permission to go).

Prioritizing Hanging Tasks

So here we are—with a brain (or planner, or sticky note) full of floaty little tasks that don't have a home yet.

You've spotted your **hanging tasks**—those to-dos that didn't make it onto your calendar, didn't earn full "King" status, but still haunt your thoughts like that one embarrassing thing you said in 7th grade.

Maybe you wrote them down somewhere.

Maybe you didn't.

Maybe you keep remembering them in the shower or at red lights.

Either way—they're **weighing you down**.

Now it's time to figure out:

What actually matters?

What can wait?

And what can *go away* with zero guilt?

Hanging Tasks Are More Than Just "Stuff to Do"

They're **unfinished loops.**

And every loop your brain is trying to keep open is one more drain on your focus, peace, and energy.

Even if the task seems small ("buy new socks," "reply to that one email," "look up allergy-friendly cupcake recipes"), it's still demanding attention. And when you've got 15 of those floating around? Of course you're exhausted. Of course your planner feels like it's never quite done.

And let's be honest: **it's not about the socks.**

It's about feeling like you're *constantly behind*, like there's always *something* you forgot, and like your brain is carrying the entire household to-do list in silent background mode—*because it probably is.*

Real Life: When Everything Feels Important

Let's talk about that mental tug-of-war you might be having right now:

"Okay, yes—I've got hanging tasks... but what if I forget something truly important? What if I let someone down?"

Totally valid. And this is why **prioritizing** matters so much.

It helps you go from:

- "Everything feels urgent" "Actually, only a few things *are* urgent."
- "I need to do all of this right now" "I can space this out over the week."

- "I keep forgetting and remembering and forgetting again" "It's in my plan. I've got this."

Prioritizing is *not* about ignoring things.

It's about putting things in their *right* place—so you can stop carrying them *all* the time.

A Quick Word for the Moms

As a mom, this can be even trickier.

Because half the hanging tasks aren't even *yours*—they're tied to your kids, your partner, your household, or other people's expectations.

Like:

- "Sign up for snacks for the Valentine's party"
- "Print out that one permission slip"
- "Remember to send Aunt Carol a thank-you card from the kids"
- "Refill the pet meds"
- "Set up the parent-teacher conference thing... again."

These feel like small things—*and yet* they're the things that will keep you awake at night, wondering what you're forgetting.

Which is why *you need a system to sort them*, fast and guilt-free.

Why Prioritizing Hanging Tasks Feels Like Mental Decluttering

Imagine you walked into a room filled with loose papers, random laundry, half-eaten snacks, and one shoe.

That's what your brain feels like with too many hanging tasks. It's cluttered. You can't think straight. And even though nothing's on fire... you kind of want to scream.

When you sit down and actually **sort those tasks by urgency and importance**, you're Marie Kondo-ing your mental space. You're saying:

"This matters today. This can wait. This doesn't belong in my mental space at all."

And suddenly? You can breathe.

This Is About More Than a Clean Planner

This is about **self-trust.**

When you start making confident decisions about what needs your time (and what doesn't), you build trust with yourself. You stop second-guessing. You stop overcommitting. You stop living in panic mode.

That's the heart of Sketch Planning.

Not cramming in more...

...but making space for what *really* matters—and *finally letting go* of what doesn't.

Scheduling Hanging Tasks

So you've done the hard part—you spotted the floaters, sorted the guilt from the goals, and faced that list of tasks that have been haunting your planner, sticky notes, and mental side tabs.

Gold star for that. Seriously.

Now comes the part that *actually moves the needle*—**placing those hanging tasks inside your Time Blocks.**

Not just thinking, *"I'll do this later."*

Not hoping you'll magically find time between laundry and school pickup.

We're giving each one a real home—so it stops floating and finally gets done.

Why Hanging Tasks Need a Home

If a task doesn't have a time, it doesn't have a chance.

When you take a task from the "mental loop" list and actually **place it into a block**, it goes from:

"Ugh, I keep forgetting this..."

to

"Cool, I'll take care of it Thursday afternoon during admin time."

That's the power of Sketch Planning—you're not just reacting. You're **assigning, anchoring, and reclaiming** your attention.

1: Match the Task to the Right Type of Block

Start by asking: *What kind of task is this, and when do I have space for it?*

Examples:

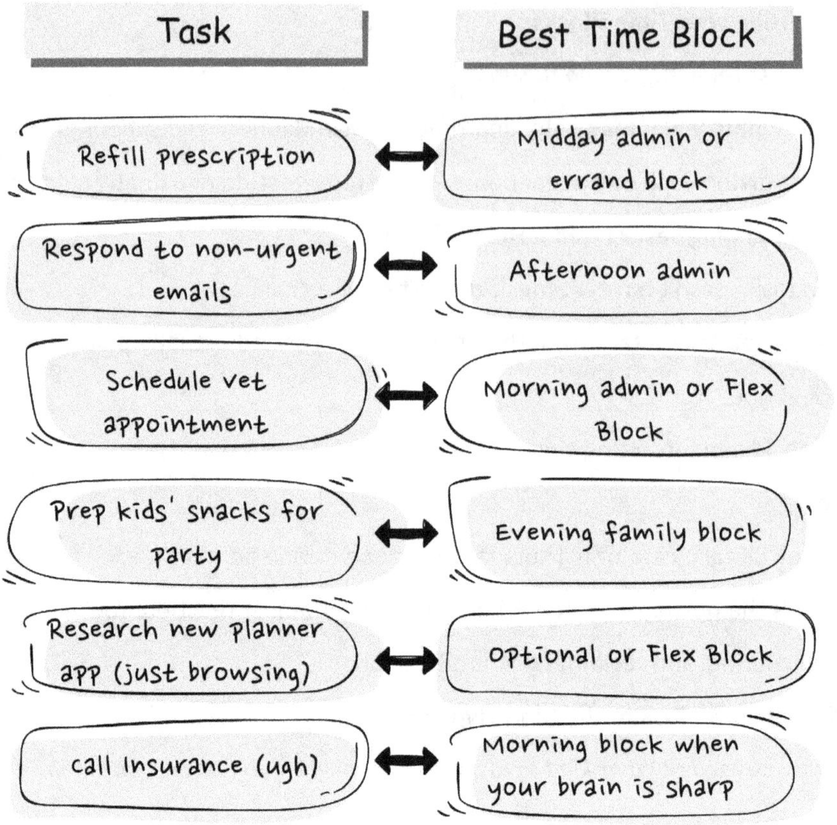
Task
Best Time Block
Refill prescription
Midday admin or errand block
Respond to non-urgent emails
Afternoon admin
Schedule vet appointment
Morning admin or Flex Block
Prep kids' snacks for party
Evening family block
Research new planner app (just browsing)
Optional or Flex Block
call Insurance (ugh)
Morning block when your brain is sharp

You're not forcing it—you're *matching* the energy and time it needs to the time and energy you actually have.

2: Batch Hanging Tasks for Efficiency

Instead of scattering tasks all over the week, **group similar hanging tasks into the same block**.

This saves time, minimizes context-switching, and gives you a solid sense of accomplishment.

Examples of batching:

- **Admin Block** respond to messages, pay bills, reschedule appointments

- **Errand Block** drop off returns, pick up prescriptions, Target run
- **Digital Block** upload files, clean up inbox, schedule social posts
- **Home Block** fold laundry, organize pantry, wipe down mystery goo in the fridge

Every Friday afternoon, I have a light Admin/Errand block. That's where my weird little tasks go—like canceling subscriptions, ordering birthday gifts, and updating spreadsheets. I've stopped trying to "squeeze them in" on heavy days, and now they actually *get done.*

3: Use a Micro Block for Quickies

Have a bunch of hanging tasks that take 5–15 minutes each?

Try a **Micro Block**—just 30–60 minutes set aside to power through a bunch of mini-tasks.

It's the "brain dump cleanup" hour.

Great for Friday afternoons, low-energy mornings, or when you need a little win.

Pro Tip: Pair it with a timer and your favorite playlist. Make it feel like a sprint, not a slog.

4: Don't Overpack Your Blocks

This one's big: **just because the task fits on the page doesn't mean it fits in your day.**

Each block should:

- Include no more than 3–5 meaningful tasks
- Have breathing room for interruptions, breaks, or slower moments
- Leave space for unexpected life things (because they *will* happen)

Sketch Planning rule: If placing a hanging task makes the block feel tight, **bump it**. It's not about stuffing—it's about flowing.

5: Use Visual Reminders (Optional but Amazing)

Once a hanging task is placed, give it a visual cue in your planner, app, or sticky note system:

- Checkboxes for satisfaction
- Icons to track urgency
- Highlighting to remind you "hey, this was hanging before—don't ignore it again!"

Or just give yourself a fun emoji reward when you finally finish that one task that's been following you for weeks

Bonus: Place One "Hanger" Per Block

Still feeling overwhelmed by the volume of your list? Try this:

One hanging task per block until they're gone.

This way, you're not derailing your day—you're gently working through your list with intention and momentum.

By week's end, most of them will be gone.

By next week? You'll be ahead of your floating to-dos *before they even start hovering.*

Don't Let Tasks Float—Help Them Land

Your plan works when your tasks have a home.

Even the little ones.

Even the ones you don't love.

Even the ones you've ignored for two weeks (or two months—no judgment).

When you place them into your Time Blocks, they stop being stressors and start being simple checkmarks.

That's how you lighten your mental load, clear the clutter, and make space for what *really* matters.

Delegating or Eliminating Hanging Tasks

Let's be real for a second.

A lot of the reason your to-do list feels overwhelming isn't because it's full of huge, high-pressure items.

It's because it's packed with **small, low-value tasks**—the kind that sneak onto your mental clipboard when you weren't looking.

Stuff like:

- Finding a new label printer (even though yours still technically works)
- Buying a birthday gift for a third cousin's kid you've never met
- Updating your Google profile photo because you "look tired in the old one"
- Scrubbing behind the washer because someone on Instagram said it sparks joy

These are *not emergencies.*

They're not even always *important.*

But they hang around—sucking energy, time, and headspace—because we've never stopped to ask the two most powerful questions in planning:

"Does this need to be done?"

"Do *I* need to be the one doing it?"

If the answer to either is "no"—then guess what?

You're free to delegate it, delay it, or delete it entirely.

And that, my friend, is where your schedule finally starts to breathe.

The Mental Load You Don't See

As women—especially moms—we're conditioned to take it all on.

We don't even realize it sometimes.

It's just... expected. Normal. Baked into the background of our lives.

So what happens?

We say things like:

- "It's easier if I just do it."
- "It won't get done right if I don't handle it."
- "It's not a big deal—I'll squeeze it in."
- "It'll only take a second."

But the truth? **Your brain is carrying too many tabs open**—and most of them aren't even tasks that need *your* attention.

Those hanging tasks that won't go away? Some of them *were never yours to carry in the first place.*

And others? They mattered once... but they don't anymore. And yet, we keep carrying them out of habit, guilt, or fear of letting someone down.

These Tasks Sneak In Because You're Trying to Be "On Top of It All"

You're not just the scheduler. You're the:

- Gift buyer
- Form filler-outer
- Email responder
- Reminder keeper
- Planner for holidays and dentist appointments and all the life things

And honestly? That's a lot.

So when a hanging task shows up, your default is probably, *"Okay, I'll take care of that."*

But what if... you didn't?

What if you got to the end of the week with fewer checkboxes—but more peace?

That's what we're doing here.

This isn't just time management. This is load management.

Real Life: The Task You Didn't Know You Could Let Go

My moment of clarity:

One day, I was redoing a printable PDF for a blog post I hadn't promoted in over a year. No one asked for it. It wasn't broken. But I thought, *"It could look better."*

I paused and asked, *"Why am I doing this right now?"*

And you know what? I stopped.

I added a note to revisit it *if* I relaunch that post, and I moved on.

The world didn't fall apart. And I got back an hour of my life.

Why We Resist Delegating or Deleting

Let's name it:

- Guilt: *"I said I'd do this."*
- Control: *"No one else will do it right."*
- Perfectionism: *"If I don't handle it, it won't be good enough."*
- Habit: *"I've always done this."*
- People-pleasing: *"They're counting on me."*

But here's the deal: when you keep everything on your plate, you don't leave room for what *actually matters*—to you, your goals, or your peace of mind.

And if that's not a good enough reason to delegate or delete something? I don't know what is.

The Power Move: Editing Your List With Authority

Every time you decide, *"This isn't mine to do,"*

or *"This doesn't need to happen at all,"*

you're making a powerful choice:

To protect your time

To respect your energy

To take the weight off your brain

You're not quitting. You're not giving up.

You're **leading** your life, like a capable, strategic CEO.

That's not lazy. That's wise.

When You Let Go, You Make Room

When you remove the unnecessary and share the workload:

- You feel lighter

- Your plan feels clearer
- Your energy rebounds
- You stop dreading your list
- And suddenly... you have space to *breathe* again

That's the goal of Sketch Planning.

Not a perfectly executed schedule, but a rhythm that actually *serves you*—not drains you.

You're Not Failing by Doing Less

You're getting strategic.

You're setting boundaries.

You're choosing what really matters—and releasing what doesn't.

And in this season? That's not just okay.

That's what thriving looks like.

Preventing Hanging Tasks

How to stop the floaters before they even start.

You've cleared the backlog.

You've scheduled what matters.

You've let go of the noise.

Now you're looking at your beautiful, clear-ish schedule and thinking:

"Please let it stay like this..."

And that's exactly what this section is about—**keeping it that way**.

Because if you're anything like most of us, the hanging tasks don't show up because you're careless or lazy (quite the opposite, honestly).

They show up because you're doing too much mental juggling with too little support.

Your brain becomes a revolving door for small to-dos:

"Don't forget to move the laundry."

"Email the teacher."

"Refill the dog's prescription."

"Schedule that mammogram."

"Check the coupon code before Friday."

"Grab napkins for the class party."

...and so on, until you're overloaded, and yet nothing feels "big enough" to block time for.

That's the trap. And the only way out?

Stop letting your brain carry the whole system.

You need habits that catch the tasks *before* they turn into clutter.

This Isn't Just Planning—It's Brain Maintenance

Here's the truth: Your brain is a brilliant idea generator.

A pattern recognizer. A decision maker. A nurturer. A problem solver.

What it's *not* meant to be?

An all-day, 24/7 reminder app.

Every unplaced task you try to "just remember" burns bandwidth.

And the more tabs you keep open in your head, the more exhausted you feel—even if you haven't "done" that much.

So the real goal here isn't more productivity.

It's **mental freedom**.

You want a system that catches the tasks *for you*—so your brain can go back to thinking, dreaming, solving, and being present.

Why the Old Way Doesn't Work

Before Sketch Planning, you might've been doing some combination of:

- Writing things on sticky notes, whiteboards, receipts, or your hand
- Repeating to-dos in your head 20 times so you wouldn't forget
- Telling your partner, *"Remind me later..."* (spoiler: they never do)
- Assuming you'll "just remember" (spoiler: you won't)
- Panicking when something falls through the cracks and promising to "be more organized next time"

This isn't a willpower problem.

It's a *system* problem.

Let's build you a system that's gentle, flexible, and actually works with your life.

Think of These as Your "Hanging Task Guardrails"

Here's the visual:

Your Time Blocks are the road.

Your Kings are the priority destinations.

Your Easily Moved tasks are your roadside stops.

And your *hanging task guardrails*? They keep the stragglers from falling into the ditch and turning into mental chaos.

Let's set those guardrails in place.

Create a "Brain Inbox" (Your Task Catcher)

Think of this as your personal front desk.

Anytime a new task, thought, or reminder pops up—*drop it here first.*

What it could look like:

- A running list in your Notes app
- A sticky note pad at your kitchen counter
- A designated notebook or section in your planner
- A voice memo or smart assistant (like, "Hey Siri, remind me...")

The key: **Everything goes here.**

Not most things. Not "the important ones."

All the things.

You don't have to decide what to do with it right away.

You just have to *catch it.*

Run a Weekly "Sketch & Sweep" Session

Set aside 15–20 minutes once a week to:

- Review your Brain Inbox
- Schedule, delegate, or delete each task
- Move important ones into Time Blocks
- Park non-urgent ideas on your "Let It Sit" list

You can combine this with your Weekly Sketch Planning session (hello, Sunday night iced caramel macchiato), or do it Friday afternoon when you're winding down.

I do mine Sunday nights while the kids argue over which show to rewatch. I light a candle, scroll my Brain Inbox, and map out my top 3 Kings for the week. Anything that doesn't fit gets slotted into a buffer block—or dumped. It's weirdly therapeutic.

Assign *Every* Task a Destination (No More Mental Maybes)

This one's key:

Once a task enters your system, it needs a *next step.*

Options:

- Schedule it into a Time Block
- Assign it to someone else
- Move it to your Flex Block
- Add it to your "Next Week" planning section
- Or delete it if it's not necessary

What you **don't** do? Let it sit "unsure" on the edge of your planner or brain space.

Hanging tasks thrive in indecision.

So give them a job—or a ticket out.

Leave Space for the Unexpected

Build intentional breathing room into your schedule every week:

- One Flex Block
- One Light Day
- One "Buffer Hour"

You don't have to be busy every second.

In fact, the more margin you build in, the better you handle those "Oh crap, I forgot to..." moments—because you actually have *space* to respond.

Watch Your Patterns Like a Detective

Still seeing certain tasks hang around week after week?

That's your cue to ask:

- Why do I keep avoiding this?
- Is this actually a priority—or a guilt task?
- Does this belong to me, or can I let it go?
- Can I break this into a smaller or delegate it?

Repeating tasks don't need more discipline.

They need a deeper look—and sometimes, a gentler plan.

Proactive = Peaceful

You don't have to juggle all the things.

You don't have to carry it all in your head.

You *do* get to:

- Build a system that protects your mental energy
- Catch and place tasks with intention
- Say "not right now" (or "not ever") without guilt
- And walk through your week feeling calm, clear, and in control

Sketch Planning doesn't just give you a better to-do list.

It gives you back the space to be present—for your work, your family, your rest, and your joy.

6

Building a Consistent Routine: Making Sketch Planning a Habit

Preventing Hanging Tasks

You've got your Sketch Planning tools.

You've mapped your Time Blocks.

You've scheduled your Kings, Easily Moved (hanging) Tasks, and you're finally starting to feel a little more in control of your day-to-day...

So how do you *keep* that momentum going?

Answer: You build a daily ritual that helps you reset, refocus, and move through your day with intention.

We're not talking about a two-hour morning routine with yoga, journaling, and hand-ground artisan coffee. (Unless that's your thing—in which case, go off .)

We're talking about a **simple, repeatable check-in** with yourself and your plan—something you can do even in sweatpants, with a messy bun, and a kid asking you where their socks are.

What Is a Sketch Planning Ritual?

It's a short, daily moment where you:

1. Review what's on your plate
2. Confirm or adjust your priorities
3. Sketch out your day using your Time Blocks
4. Mentally walk through what's coming
5. Decide what needs to happen—and what can wait

Think of it as giving your day a map.

Even if the road gets bumpy, you'll know where you're headed—and what matters most.

Why a Daily Ritual Works (Even If Your Days Don't Always Go to Plan)

A daily ritual gives you:

- **Clarity:** You know what you're doing and *why*
- **Focus:** You stop chasing every shiny object or sudden "urgent" thing
- **Confidence:** You're making intentional choices instead of reacting
- **Calm:** Your brain can chill because it knows you're in charge

Even when life throws curveballs (which it always does), having a ritual helps you pivot without spiraling.

When to Do It: Morning, Night, or Both?

This totally depends on your energy, brain type, and season of life.

Morning Sketch Ritual:

- Best for: Moms who need to ground themselves *before* the chaos hits
- When: After drop-off, during your first cup of coffee, or before opening your laptop
- Bonus: It's a mindset reset. You start your day in control, instead of playing catch-up.

Evening Sketch Ritual:

- Best for: Night owls, overthinkers, or moms who need to mentally "close the tab" before bed
- When: After dinner, before TV time, while the kids are getting ready for the next day
- Bonus: It sets up tomorrow *before* tomorrow starts. You wake up feeling clear, not frantic.

Most nights, I do a mini sketch session while the girls get ready for bed. I review what happened that day, carry over anything that needs rescheduling, and sketch out my Kings and blocks for tomorrow. Sometimes it takes 10 minutes, sometimes just 3—but it always makes the next day feel less intimidating.

What to Include in Your Daily Sketch Planning Ritual

Customize this to fit your life—but here's a simple structure to start with:

The Daily Sketch Checklist:

What are my top 1–3 Kings for the day?

What Time Blocks do I have today, and what's already scheduled in them?

Do I have any hanging tasks (Easily Moved) that need a home?

Is there a Flex Block or buffer time I can use if something pops up?

Am I feeling overwhelmed—or is this plan doable?

What *doesn't* need to happen today?

Write it down. Say it out loud. Tap it into your planner app. Whatever works for your brain is the right way.

Keep It Light, Keep It Flexible

This isn't a pressure ritual. It's a *permission* ritual.

Some days, you'll feel laser-focused and ready to conquer the world.

Other days, you'll move one King to another block and call it good.

Both count. Both are wins.

The point is to *keep checking in* with your plan and your energy—so you're always working with yourself, not against yourself.

Bonus Ritual Boosters (Optional, But Fun)

If you want to make it feel a little more *you*, try:

- Lighting a candle or turning on a calming playlist
- Pairing it with your favorite
- Using stickers or colored pens to make your planner feel like a happy place
- Writing a quick "what worked today" or "what I'm proud of" note

You don't need these to succeed—but a little joy in your routine never hurts.

A Ritual Makes It *Real*

Planning isn't something you do once and forget.

It's a relationship—with your time, your energy, and your priorities.

A daily Sketch Planning ritual helps you nurture that relationship, little by little, until it becomes second nature.

You don't have to do it perfectly.

You just have to *show up for it.*

Even three minutes a day can be the difference between drowning in your to-dos... and moving through them with peace and power.

Setting Realistic Goals

Let's stop chasing perfection and start building real, doable momentum.

If there's one thing moms are *really* good at—it's setting the bar higher than it needs to be.

We wake up with a mental list like:

- Pack lunches
- Prep dinner
- Reply to emails
- Keep a toddler alive
- Take dog to vet
- Launch a course
- Organize the garage

- Start that "fun" craft project we saw on Pinterest
- Oh, and also *drink water* and *take care of ourselves* because #balance

By 10 a.m., we're either exhausted, behind, or totally off-track because one unexpected curveball (like a mystery rash or an "I forgot my Chromebook" phone call from school) blew it all up.

So we throw our hands up, say "I'll start over tomorrow," and silently beat ourselves up for not getting it all done.

Sound familiar?

The truth is: **it's not you. It's the pressure.**

Most women—especially busy moms and multi-hat-wearers—don't struggle with motivation.

We struggle with **overcommitment**, **unrealistic expectations**, and **a chronic underestimation of how long stuff actually takes**.

So let's reframe what goal-setting looks like with Sketch Planning.

Let's make it doable, gentle, and *honest*—so we can *finally feel good about what we're doing* instead of guilty about what we're not.

First: Why Realistic Goals Actually *Fuel* Motivation

We think motivation comes from ambition.

But it actually comes from momentum.

And you know what kills momentum faster than anything?

A goal that's way too big

A plan that ignores your actual life

A list that has 14 "non-negotiables"

When your goals are unreachable, your brain sees "failure" before you even start.

It shuts down. You avoid the list. Then you feel worse.

Realistic goals do the opposite.

They build confidence.

They give you wins.

And those wins keep you showing up again and again.

The Cycle Most Women Are Stuck In

Here's the typical pattern:

1. **You get excited.** You write a big list or set a big weekly goal.
2. **You try to do it all.** You pack your blocks, juggle too many Kings, skip your Flex space.
3. **Something unexpected happens.** (It always does.)
4. **You fall behind.** You either panic or freeze.
5. **You blame yourself.** You question your worth, your abilities, your systems.
6. **You vow to "try harder" next time.**
7. **Repeat.**

Sketch Planning is here to interrupt that cycle and offer something new:

A system that *accepts your humanity*—and still gets stuff done.

The Reframe: "What Would Success Look Like Today?"

Instead of asking:

"How much can I cram into this day?"

Try asking:

"What one or two things would make me feel proud at the end of today?"

This changes everything. It lowers pressure while raising intentionality.

You're not abandoning goals.

You're choosing *alignment over achievement.*

Big difference.

The Mini Goal Mindset Shift

You don't have to get everything done.

You just need to keep moving forward in a way that works *for you.*

Try this mindset reframe when sketching goals:

Momentum > Magnitude. Every single time.

Real Life Example: My "Not Today" Moments

There are days when my list looks amazing. Color-coded. Prioritized. Full of potential.

And then… the dog throws up.

The power blips.

The house is a mess.

Someone needs emotional support.

Or my brain just decides it needs a soft day.

I used to feel like a failure when I couldn't keep up with my own goals.

Now? I resketch.

I drop one King, lean on my Flex Block, or bump a task to next week—*on purpose*.

That's not quitting.

That's knowing myself.

That's mature, strategic planning. And it's what keeps me showing up.

Motivation Tip: Track *How You Feel* After Each Day

Forget measuring success by how many boxes you check.

Try asking:

- Did I follow through on what mattered?
- Did I feel rushed, or steady?
- Did I adjust with grace instead of guilt?
- Did I protect my peace—even just a little?

When you start defining success by how a plan *supports* your life—not how hard you hustle—you'll stop needing willpower... and start having real, lasting motivation.

Do Less to Go Further

Setting realistic goals isn't giving up on your dreams.

It's giving your dreams a real chance to grow—without burning you out along the way.

You don't need to do everything today.

You just need to do the right things, in the right rhythm, for the season you're in.

That's how you build sustainable success.

That's how you stay motivated.

That's how you *finally feel proud of your plan.*

Tracking Progress

Because celebrating wins is just as important as planning them.

You've been sketching your days.

You've been identifying Kings.

You've delegated, deleted, shifted, adjusted, and slowly started feeling a little more on top of things.

Now what?

Now, we check in.

Because the magic of Sketch Planning doesn't come from doing it *perfectly* every day.

It comes from **building awareness over time**—about what's working, what's not, and where you're ready to grow.

Let's walk through how to track your progress in a way that motivates—not shames—you.

First, Why Track Your Progress At All?

Because most of us are way too hard on ourselves.

You might be doing *really well*—but without a moment to reflect, you miss it.

Instead, you focus on what you didn't finish. What got bumped. What still feels messy.

Tracking your progress helps you:

- **Celebrate wins you'd otherwise overlook**
- **Spot patterns** (good *and* not-so-good)
- **Make smarter decisions about your time**
- **Stay encouraged—even when things feel slow**
- **Build trust with yourself**

This isn't a performance review. It's a *kind accountability practice* that supports you.

1: Choose How You Want to Track

This can be *super simple* or as detailed as you want.

Low-key options:

- A weekly "What Went Well" list

- Daily checkmark system for completed Kings
- Sticky notes with one win per day
- A bullet journal spread with color coding for mood vs. progress

More structured ideas:

- A Google Doc or Notion page for weekly reflections
- A printable tracker with sections like: "Wins," "Adjustments," "Next Week's Focus"
- A digital form you fill out each Friday to review the week

My go-to:

I jot down three things at the end of the week:

1. What worked well
2. What felt heavy
3. One thing I want to try differently next week
4. It's handwritten in my planner—nothing fancy, just real and quick.

2: Define What "Success" Means for You

Don't let the world define it.

You get to decide what *matters*.

Some weeks success looks like:

- Launching something new
- Getting through a rough week without melting down

- Following your Time Blocks 60% of the time
- Finishing one King each day
- Letting go of guilt when things had to move

Ask yourself:

"What would I be proud of this week—even if no one else saw it?"

That's the real metric.

3: Look for Patterns—Not Perfection

When you reflect, you're not just checking boxes. You're looking for **clues**.

Ask:

- Which Time Blocks consistently feel good?
- Which ones feel too packed or get skipped often?
- What kinds of tasks keep floating? (Ahem... repeat hanging tasks)
- Are there days I feel energized vs. drained?
- Did my goals match my energy and schedule—or not really?

This isn't about judgment.

It's about **getting curious**.

If something keeps slipping, it doesn't mean you failed—it means it might need a new home, a new approach, or less pressure.

4: Track Your Energy, Not Just Your Tasks

Especially if you're a mom, a business owner, or a human dealing with unpredictable life stuff—**your energy matters more than your output.**

Try adding a super simple energy check-in to your week:

What tasks lit me up?

What totally drained me?

When did I feel mentally checked out—and why?

Use those answers to adjust *how* you plan your week.

It's okay to lean into what feels good and back from what feels heavy.

Energy isn't selfish—it's **strategy**.

5: Make Celebration Part of the Process

One of the biggest reasons we lose momentum?

We forget to celebrate.

So please—track the little wins, the effort, the intention. Not just the results.

You finished 3 out of 5 Kings? Celebrate.

You actually *used* your Flex Block this week? Celebrate.

You remembered to sketch three days in a row? *Big win.*

We don't grow from pressure. We grow from *recognition.*

Sketch Planning isn't just about moving forward—it's about feeling good while you do it.

Progress > Perfection

You don't need to track everything.

But you *do* deserve a moment to reflect, reset, and remind yourself that you're doing better than you think.

The only way to grow with Sketch Planning is to pay attention—not to how perfect your plan was, but to how well it supported your life.

You're not trying to prove anything.

You're just learning, adjusting, and becoming someone who *trusts herself* with her time.

That's real progress.

And it's worth celebrating every single week.

Celebrating Successes

Because if you don't stop to notice your progress, your brain will convince you there wasn't any.

Here's something most women aren't taught:

You are allowed to feel proud of yourself *before everything is perfect.*

That half-finished list? Still worth celebrating.

That one hard thing you got done even though the rest fell apart? Still matters.

That quiet win no one else sees? Still deserves your attention.

But most of us don't.

Because we've been trained to believe we only deserve to celebrate when the list is done, the inbox is zero, the launch is live, the house is clean, and the kids are fed something other than cereal.

So we delay joy. We delay recognition. We wait until it's "all caught up" to feel good about ourselves—which, let's be honest, never really happens.

Sketch Planning flips that mindset on its head.

It says: *Celebrate the doing. Celebrate the trying. Celebrate the clarity. Celebrate showing up.*

And watch what happens when you do.

Why We Forget to Celebrate

Let's name it:

- We're too focused on what we didn't finish
- We're always thinking about the next task
- We think celebrating means we're slacking off
- We feel like we're not "doing enough" to deserve it
- We're waiting for someone else to recognize us

But here's the truth: **If you only celebrate perfection, you'll never feel satisfied.**

That's a hamster wheel. It'll wear you down.

What you need—and what Sketch Planning builds into your workflow—is space to recognize *real progress* in *real life.*

Progress Doesn't Have to Be Big to Be Worth Celebrating

Here's what counts:

- Moving a task on purpose instead of forgetting it
- Stopping before burnout hits
- Finishing your top King and letting the rest wait
- Sketching your plan two days in a row (even if day three went off the rails)
- Remembering your kid's library day this week
- Saying no without explaining
- Choosing a frozen pizza instead of forcing a "real" meal—because you needed rest

This is not laziness. This is *leadership* of your time, energy, and attention.

What Happens When You Start Celebrating

You stop associating planning with shame.

You stop thinking, *"I'm behind,"* and start thinking, *"I'm learning."*

You stop needing external validation and start trusting yourself to notice growth.

This is the beginning of **sustainable motivation**—the kind that doesn't rely on hustle, hype, or a perfect streak.

It comes from *knowing your own progress and honoring it.*

A Mom-Life Note: You're Doing More Than You Think

If you're a mom, you're carrying an invisible load every day.

That "nothing got done today" feeling? It's often a lie.

You:

- Solved 19 minor crises before lunch
- Fed people (possibly multiple species)
- Responded to 43 interruptions
- Helped with homework while managing a business
- Held space for someone else's big emotions
- Got everyone out the door without losing your mind (or at least tried)

So even when your Kings didn't get crossed off... you still showed up.

You still *mothered.* That matters. That counts.

There are days I don't even touch my computer until 4 p.m. because of life, appointments, and everything else. I used to beat myself up for that. Now, I celebrate when I sketch out a recovery plan instead of spiraling. That is progress. That is strength.

Celebration Doesn't Have to Be Fancy—Just Felt

Try any of these:

- Say out loud: *"I'm proud of myself today."*
- Write down one win before bed (no matter how small)
- Do a little happy dance or victory stretch
- Light a candle when you finish a King task
- Make a "Win Jar" with sticky notes you can read when you're low
- Text a friend: *"I did the thing!"*
- Tell your kids: *"Mom crushed a goal today!"* and let them cheer for you

Your nervous system *needs* these moments.

It resets your brain's default setting from "not enough" to "doing just fine."

What to Say to Yourself

You don't need permission to celebrate.

But if you've been waiting for someone to hand it to you—here it is:

"I didn't finish everything, but I finished what mattered."

"I'm proud of how I adjusted when the day went sideways."

"I stayed flexible and focused—that's a win."

"I said no to something that didn't align."

"I made space for rest, and that counts."

Your plan is not a test. It's a tool.

Your progress isn't a report card. It's a rhythm.

Recognize What's Working—So You Can Keep Going

The best way to maintain momentum isn't pushing harder.

It's pausing to *notice* what you're already doing well.

Sketch Planning doesn't just give you a way to stay on track.

It gives you **a reason to feel good about the track you're on.**

So celebrate the baby steps.

Celebrate the pivots.

Celebrate the growth no one else sees.

This is how you build a life that works—with less shame, more celebration, and a lot more joy in the journey.

Adapting Your Routine

Because your life changes—and your plan should too.

So here you are.

You've mapped your Time Blocks.

You're using Sketch Planning to manage your Kings, keep tasks from floating, and (finally!) stay one ahead of overwhelm.

Things are flowing. You're in a groove.

But then... something shifts.

- Your kids start a new school schedule
- You launch a new project or business
- You start working different hours

- A family member needs more support
- Or maybe you just feel *different*—tired, stretched, uninspired

Suddenly, the system that felt so perfect a month ago feels... clunky. Frustrating. Off.

Sound familiar?

Here's the truth: **this doesn't mean your routine is broken.**

It means you're evolving. And your plan needs to evolve with you.

Why Routines Need to Shift (Even When They're Working)

A planning system is like a great pair of jeans—it fits amazingly well... until life changes shape.

And life *always* changes shape.

That's why routines should be **living, breathing frameworks**—not rigid rules.

Your Sketch Planning system is built for this. It's not about locking in the perfect day forever. It's about knowing how to adjust *with intention* instead of falling into chaos or burnout.

1: Recognize the Signals That It's Time to Adapt

Not sure if your routine needs a refresh? Look for these signs:

- You're skipping or dreading your planning ritual
- You keep running out of time in the same block every day
- You feel behind even though you're working hard
- Your tasks don't match your energy or capacity anymore
- You're planning like a robot but living like a human

Basically, if your plan feels like pressure—not support—it's time for a little sketch tune-up.

2: Re-Sketch—Don't Scrap

When your routine stops working, the goal isn't to throw everything out.

It's to ask, *"What's no longer serving me—and what still is?"*

Use this simple 3-column reflection:

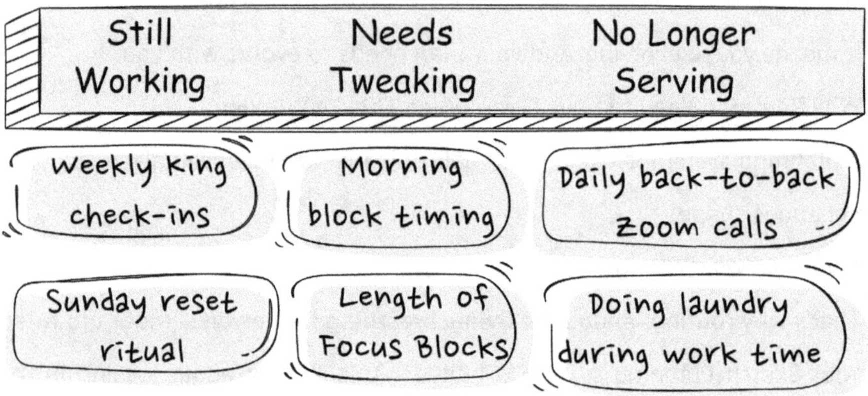
Still Working
Needs Tweaking
No Longer Serving
Weekly king check-ins
Morning block timing
Daily back-to-back zoom calls
Sunday reset ritual
Length of Focus Blocks
Doing laundry during work time

This gives you clarity without drama.

My truth:

When my youngest started a new school, our mornings shifted hard. I had been doing deep work early—but now, I needed a buffer just to recover from carline drama. Instead of forcing old habits, I rebuilt my blocks to reflect the new flow. Was it perfect? Nope. But it was *real*—and that made all the difference.

3: Modify Blocks with Your Current Life in Mind

Once you've identified what needs adjusting, try modifying just **one or two blocks** at a time:

- Make your morning block shorter (if your energy is lower)
- Add a 30-min "transition" block between parenting and work

- Create a new Weekly Focus Block instead of daily ones
- Move admin tasks to your low-energy times
- Insert a midday rest block and stop calling it "lazy"

Small shifts = big impact. You don't need a full overhaul. You just need alignment.

4: Practice Seasonal Planning

Sometimes, your routine just needs to change with the season—literally *and* metaphorically.

Try asking every quarter:

- What season am I *in* right now? (Life-wise, not just weather-wise)
- What does my energy look like?
- What responsibilities are shifting?
- What boundaries do I need to reset?
- What's inspiring me right now—and what's draining me?

Then adjust your blocks and goals accordingly.

Because planning for summer break doesn't look like planning for back-to-school.

And postpartum routines don't look like pre-baby workflows.

And launch weeks don't look like recovery weeks.

Sketch Planning honors your seasons. It flexes so you don't have to break.

5: Build Re-Sketching Into Your Routine

Make adaptation *part* of the system by checking in every month or quarter with:

What's working in my current routine?

What's feeling too tight or too loose?

Do I need more rest? More structure? More support?

What do I need *less* of?

This prevents burnout and keeps you connected to your goals *and* your capacity.

You're not starting over—you're stepping forward with wisdom.

You Are Allowed to Change

You don't have to plan like the version of you from three months ago.

You don't have to feel guilty for needing more margin.

You're growing. Your life is shifting. And your plan should shift with you.

Sketch Planning isn't about building the perfect routine—it's about creating a flexible one.

One that bends with your reality, supports your peace, and helps you stay focused on what matters *right now.*

So go ahead—re-sketch. Reinvent. Reclaim your rhythm.

Your plan will still be here, cheering you on.

7

Planning for Work: Optimizing Professional Productivity

Prioritizing Work Tasks

Because your business, job, or dream deserves structure that feels like support—not pressure.

Here's the thing no one talks about when you're balancing work and life:

You're never *just* working.

You're also:

- Managing a house
- Managing a family
- Remembering birthdays
- Keeping track of library books and softball cleats

- Getting food on the table
- Answering work emails between loads of laundry or lunchbox assembly

And somehow, you're also supposed to set ambitious goals, build a career, maybe grow a business, and stay "productive" like you're a robot on caffeine and 6 hours of sleep.

It's exhausting.

And traditional time management systems don't account for the real mess of modern mom-life-work-life integration.

Sketch Planning does.

Because it's flexible enough to hold *both* sides of your day—and wise enough to help you **prioritize what actually matters** in your work time, so you can stop spinning and start *making progress that feels good.*

The Dual Life of Working Moms (and Why It's Complicated)

Whether you work part-time, full-time, remotely, freelance, run a business, or are dreaming something into life while also managing carpool and dinner-time—your brain is *always on.*

You don't get to clock out at 5.

You don't always have quiet, focused time.

You're squeezing in deep work between kid drop-offs, laundry, and snack requests.

You're managing mental load *and* meeting deadlines.

And when your work list gets tangled up with your life list, everything starts to feel impossible.

That's why Sketch Planning doesn't separate "work vs. life."

It helps you sketch your time *honestly*—with both parts considered, and **your energy front and center.**

1: Define Your "Work Kings" (Yes, You Have Them)

Just like with your personal responsibilities, your professional life has its own *Kings*—those **non-negotiable, high-impact tasks** that truly move the needle forward.

They're not always flashy. But they matter.

Your Work Kings might include:

- Writing or recording new content
- Showing up for a client or customer
- Marketing or sales activity
- Training or team leadership
- Launch prep or project delivery
- Billing or backend maintenance
- Research, strategy, or innovation

The goal? Stop giving equal energy to *everything.*

Instead, pour your best focus into the work that actually grows your business, helps your clients, or builds your future.

I used to treat inbox zero like a King. But answering every email doesn't grow my business. Now, I sketch blocks for content, strategy, or promotion first—*then* admin stuff if time allows.

2: Use Your Time Blocks Like a CEO

You don't need more hours.

You need better *boundaries* around the hours you already have.

Create *dedicated* Time Blocks just for work—based on your real-life availability and energy.

Here's a sample day:

Block Name	Time Range	Focus Area
Morning Focus	8:30 - 11:00	Writing or high-priority deep work (Work King!)
Midday Admin	1:00 - 2:00	Emails, calls, inbox cleanup
Flex Overflow	2:00 - 3:00	Quick wins, wrap-up, or household crossover
Personal Block	3:00 - 5:00	School pickup, dinner prep, errands

This prevents overlap that drains you and sets realistic expectations for what you can *actually* get done.

Pro Tip: Labeling Time Blocks keeps your brain from bouncing between modes. When you're in a work block, be *at work*. When it ends, close that loop and return to the rest of your life with peace.

3: Sketch Work & Life Together—But Don't Let Them Compete

In Sketch Planning, we honor the fact that you don't live in two separate worlds.

That's why I recommend sketching your personal and professional Kings **side by side**.

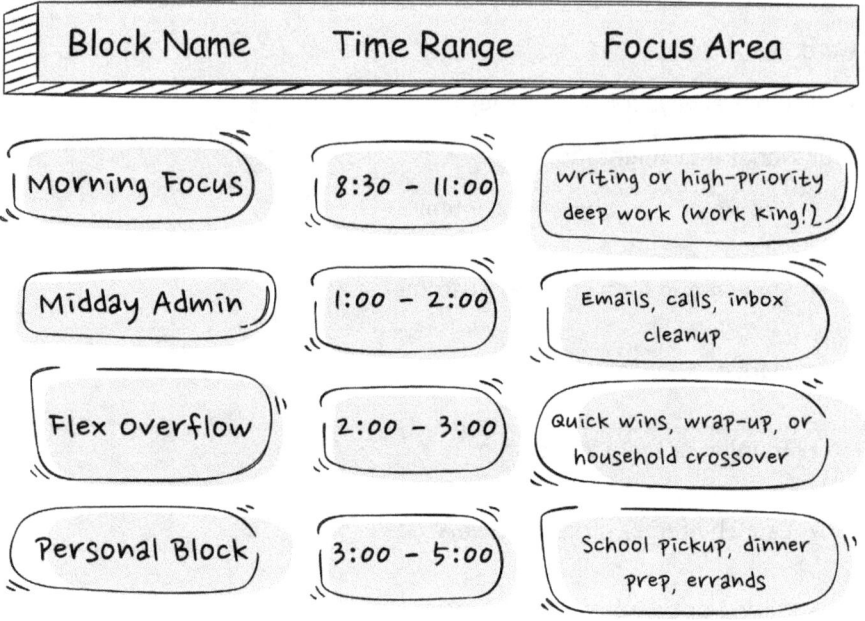

Here's an example:

Time Block	Life King	Work King
8:00 - 10:00	Drop-off & dishes	Write content for email funnel
10:00 - 12:00	-	client call & Prep notes
12:00 - 1:00	Launch & walk dog	-
1:00 - 3:00	Grocery pickup	Edit landing page & check-in with VA
3:00 - 5:00	kids home, homework	No work block planned

This way, you're seeing **your day as a whole**, not fighting against yourself because "life stuff keeps getting in the way."

Life *is* the way. Sketch around it.

4: Let Go of "Doing It All"—And Get Strategic Instead

You don't have to:

- Answer every email immediately
- Be on every platform
- Say yes to every opportunity
- Create content every single day
- Always "be available" just because you work from home

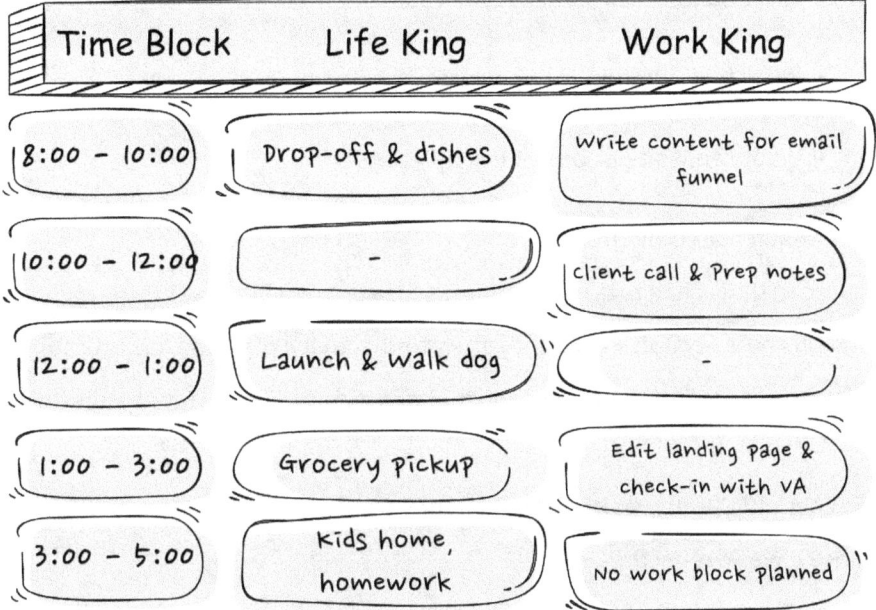

Start asking:

- What builds income, impact, or momentum?
- What feels aligned with my strengths and season?
- What can wait—or be done simpler?

Then sketch accordingly.

I used to think I had to do #allthethings to be successful. Now, I focus my Work Kings on the *essentials*—revenue-generating activity, planning, and nurturing my audience. That's it. And guess what? I get more done *and* feel better doing it.

5: Check In Weekly—Without Judgment

Once a week, reflect:

- What were my biggest work wins?
- What felt chaotic?
- Did my work blocks feel spacious or crammed?
- What should I adjust next week?

This reflection keeps your plan evolving—so it continues to support your growth instead of dragging you down.

Even a quick sticky note or voice memo can be enough. The point is to notice the patterns so you don't repeat the burnout cycle.

You Can Work Well Without Working More

Integrating your work into your Sketch Plan doesn't mean becoming superhuman.

It means getting *honest* about what matters.

It means creating space for deep focus—and for flexibility.

It means allowing your planning system to support your ambition *without overwhelming your life.*

Work doesn't have to be a fire you're constantly putting out.

It can be a calm, productive flow—when you plan it with intention, not pressure.

You've got the tools now.

You've got the rhythm.

And your work deserves the peace that Sketch Planning brings.

Managing Meetings and Deadlines

Because you shouldn't need a second brain (or six extra hours) just to get through your calendar.

If there's one thing that can derail a perfectly good Sketch Plan, it's this:

"Can you hop on a quick call?"

"We need it by EOD."

"Let's meet about that project—how's Thursday at 3?"

Suddenly your day—your beautiful, intentional day—is hijacked by Zoom invites and ticking clocks.

Here's the good news: Sketch Planning doesn't just *survive* deadlines and meetings.

It *thrives* with them—when you use Time Blocks the right way.

This section is all about keeping your work schedule clear, doable, and on-track—even when meetings pile up and deadlines sneak in.

1: Time Blocks = Containers, Not Chains

Let's start here: **Time Blocks are flexible frameworks—not rigid rules.**

They give you structure, but they also protect your mental space.

When you assign meetings or deadlines to specific blocks instead of scattering them across your day like glitter... suddenly, things feel a *lot* more manageable.

You're not "fitting in a call."

You're *placing it with purpose.*

2: Create a Dedicated "Meeting Block"

If your days are peppered with calls and check-ins, this one's a game changer.

Instead of saying yes to *any* time someone offers, carve out a recurring **Meeting Block** on your calendar.

It might look like:

- Tuesdays & Thursdays from 1–3pm
- Wednesdays from 10am–12pm
- Daily Flex Block from 2–3pm just for quick calls or meetings

Then, when someone asks, *"What works for you?"*—you already know.

You're not cramming a meeting into your only deep work window.

I protect my mornings like gold. That's where I do creative and strategic work. If someone asks to meet, I always suggest my Afternoon Meeting Block first. If it doesn't work? We move it to a different day. It keeps my focus intact and my energy steady.

3: Sketch Deadlines Into Your Week—Not Just the Due Date

Most people make this mistake:

They write down the deadline, but not the *work it takes to meet it.*

Sketch Planning helps you avoid that.

Here's how:

1. **Add the actual due date to your calendar**

2. Work backward using Time Blocks to map *prep tasks*

3. Assign specific parts of the project to specific days

For example:

Date	Task	Time Block
Monday	Outline client proposal	Morning Focus
Tuesday	Draft slides	Afternoon Block
Wednesday	Review & Finalize	Midday Block
Thursday	Submit by noon	Admin or wrap-up Block

Suddenly, you're not stressed at 11:48 a.m. on Thursday wondering how it crept up on you.

4: Use a "Deadline Buffer" Block

Build in a weekly Buffer Block just for:

- Wrapping up near-due tasks

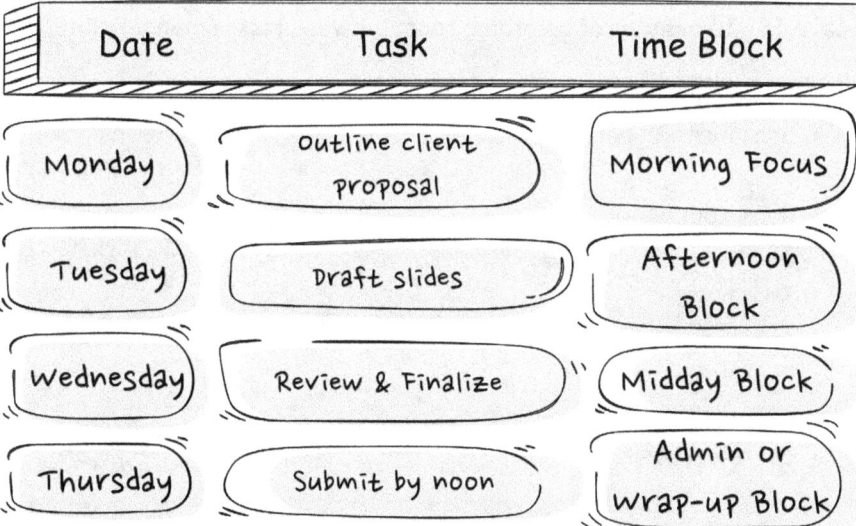

- Handling last-minute reviews
- Catching anything that got bumped midweek

This is like giving your planner a safety net.

Even just one 60-minute block on Thursday or Friday can make your week feel *so* much more manageable.

Bonus: If you don't need it for deadlines? You've got space for overflow, catch-up, or early clock-out time.

5: Avoid Back-to-Back Burnout

If your week is full of meetings and project work, don't forget this golden rule:

Leave 15–30 minutes of breathing room between tasks when possible.

Use those windows to:

- Shift mental gears
- Refill your water
- Take notes
- Review your plan
- Eat (please eat)

Sketch Planning is about real life. And real life needs margins.

6: Recap + Reset Each Week

Before your next week starts, do a quick review:

- Which meetings supported my progress?
- Which ones felt unnecessary or draining?
- Did I leave enough time to actually *do* the work in between?

- Did I hit my deadlines *without* panic?

Then use that insight to adjust next week's blocks. This is how your plan gets *smarter* over time.

You Run the Calendar—Not the Other Way Around

Meetings and deadlines aren't the enemy.

But letting them dictate your entire day without boundaries? That's where burnout begins.

Sketch Planning gives you the tools to:

- Place things *intentionally*
- Say no (or *"not at that time"*) without guilt
- Prep ahead so deadlines don't crush you
- And stay focused—without skipping lunch or collapsing at 5pm

You're not just managing time.

You're managing *energy*, *expectations*, and your *well-being*—like the capable queen you are.

Your calendar doesn't own you.

Your plan empowers you.

Handling Interruptions and Distractions

Because "just five uninterrupted minutes" is a fantasy—and we're done pretending otherwise.

You sit down with your iced caramel macchiato.

You've got your Morning Focus Block sketched.

You're ready to write, create, or finally tackle that lingering to-do...

And then it begins.

- You spill something on your one "decent" shirt
- The dog starts barking at a squirrel.
- Your phone pings with a "just checking in" text.
- Your brain decides now is the perfect time to reorganize the pantry—mentally, at least.
- Someone schedules a "quick call" at the exact time you planned to do deep work.

Welcome to working in real life.

Interruptions are inevitable.

But with Sketch Planning, they don't have to derail your entire day.

1: Sketch *with* Interruptions in Mind

Here's the mindset shift: **You don't plan to avoid interruptions—you plan to absorb them.**

That means:

- Leaving buffer space between blocks
- Using Flex Blocks as overflow for unfinished tasks
- Avoiding back-to-back focus blocks

- Assigning your hardest Work Kings to your least interruptible time of day (aka "golden windows")

Even 90% of a Time Block is more than you'd have without a plan.

When I schedule a writing block, I *know* I'll get interrupted. So I give myself 90 minutes for what technically takes 60. That way, if a snack request or school call happens, I'm not immediately stressed—I've got wiggle room built in.

2: Identify Your Personal Distraction Triggers

Interruptions aren't always external. Sometimes the call is coming from inside the house.

Common culprits:

- Email tabs left open
- Phone notifications
- Slack/DM pings
- Multitasking (the productivity killer in disguise)
- "Let me just check one thing..." (spoiler: it's never one thing)

Take 5 minutes to ask:

"What most often pulls me away from my Work Kings?"

Then put simple barriers in place:

- Turn off notifications
- Use website blockers (like Freedom or Cold Turkey)
- Work in full-screen mode
- Wear noise-canceling headphones—even if they're not plugged in

3: Pre-Decide How You'll Handle Interruptions

This is *so powerful.*

Instead of reacting in the moment, decide ahead of time:

- What interruptions are **worth pausing for** (emergencies, urgent calls)
- What can **wait until your block ends** (non-urgent texts, house chores)
- What gets **redirected completely** (e.g., "Ask Dad," "Put it on the list," "I'll handle that after 2pm")

Create a default response for each type of distraction so you're not spending energy re-deciding every time.

Try this script:

"I'm working until 10:30. Write it down, and I'll look at it then."

"Can you handle that or wait until I finish my block?"

"I'm in work mode—circle back in an hour."

And mean it. You're allowed to protect your focus.

4: Use a Visual Signal That Says "Do Not Distract"

This one is especially great for moms working at home.

Try:

- Wearing noise-canceling headphones (even if you're not listening to anything)
- Hanging a "Working—Back Soon" sign on your office door
- Using a lamp, sticky note, or signal card to indicate you're in a Focus Block
- Letting your family know *when* you'll be available next

If you're consistent, they'll (eventually) get it. And if not... you at least feel like a boss in headphones.

5: When All Else Fails—Resketch, Don't Rage Quit

There will be days when the interruptions win.

When the blender lid wasn't on. You now have smoothie *everywhere*

When someone knocks on your door right as you find your flow.

Those are not failures.

They're reminders that you're living in real life—not a Pinterest board.

So instead of spiraling or giving up, just say:

"Okay. New plan."

Re-sketch your day.

Move your Kings.

Bump the low-priority stuff.

Claim your next open block like a boss.

One Monday, I had a perfect sketch ready. Then the fridge didn't want to stay cold, the garage door wouldn't close and I got a surprise bill I had to call about. Did I get all my Kings done? Nope. But I moved one to the next day, handled what I could, and let that be enough. That's Sketch Planning in real life.

Your Focus Is Valuable—Even When It's Interrupted

You're not failing when your blocks get disrupted.

You're *winning* when you adjust and keep going without shame.

Focus isn't about perfection. It's about **returning to your priorities**, again and again, with kindness and clarity.

Sketch Planning isn't just about getting through your to-do list.

It's about **staying calm, capable, and confident in the chaos**—even when the interruptions don't stop coming.

You've got this. And the next time your focus is shattered mid-thought?

Take a deep breath. Shake it off. Re-sketch. And keep going.

Collaborating with Colleagues

Because you shouldn't have to choose between staying focused and being a team player.

One of the best things about Sketch Planning?

It gives *you* clarity on how your day flows.

One of the trickiest things about working with other humans?

They don't always respect or understand that flow.

You're mid-Work King, focused and flowing, and then a Slack message pops up:

"Got a sec?"

"Hey, random question..."

"Can you take a quick look at this real fast?"

Suddenly, your plan is in flames and you're off chasing someone else's urgency.

But here's the good news: You can use your Sketch Plan to *gently teach people how to work with you, not against you*—without being rigid or unapproachable.

Let's talk about how.

1: Share Your Work Style—Without Apologizing for It

Start by telling your team or collaborators how you work best.

You don't need to overshare or make a PowerPoint. Just try something like:

"Hey! I've been working in Time Blocks to help me stay focused and avoid task-switching burnout. I usually batch communication in the afternoon, so if you message me in the morning, I may not reply right away—but I *will* circle back!"

Or:

"Mornings are my deep work time, so I usually keep meetings to after lunch. Happy to chat then!"

It's not about building walls—it's about **setting helpful expectations.**

I tell my team: "I sketch out my top Kings each day and protect those focus blocks. If you need something urgently, text me. Otherwise, I check messages at the top of each admin block and will respond then." No one's confused, and I don't feel guilty for not being *always on.*

2: Create a Shared Calendar or "Team View" of Your Blocks

If you work closely with a team (or even a VA), try sharing a light version of your block schedule—something like:

- Mornings: Content or creative work (Do Not Disturb)

- Midday: Team comms + Admin

- Afternoons: Meetings, review, support

- Fridays: Flex + overflow

- Buffer time: 30 minutes before lunch daily

This helps others know when you're available, *without you needing to micro-manage access to your time.*

Tools like Google Calendar, Notion, or even a Slack status can work for this.

3: Use Sketch Lingo to Communicate Clearly

Once you've explained your Sketch Planning approach to your team, you can start using simple terms like:

- "That's one of my Kings this week"
- "Let's slot that into a Flex Block"
- "I'll handle that in my Admin Block tomorrow"
- "Can we move this to Friday's overflow time?"

It's short, it's clear, and it helps *everyone* prioritize and reduce last-minute scrambles.

And hey—maybe your team starts picking it up too. (Just saying… Sketch Planning revolution for everyone?)

4: Use Shared Sketching for Collaboration Sessions

You can even *co-sketch* for projects by having a quick planning huddle to map out:

- What the team's Kings are this week
- Who's owning which piece (delegation!)
- When each task will be worked on (Time Blocks!)
- Where check-ins will happen (and *not* in 18 emails)

It takes 10–15 minutes but saves hours of "Where are we at?" conversations later.

This works beautifully in team meetings, project launches, or even collaborations with affiliate partners or contractors.

5: Balance Boundaries with Flexibility

You're a team player—but that doesn't mean being available 24/7 or sacrificing your priorities for someone else's panic.

When you do need to bend your blocks:

- Acknowledge it ("Not my usual block, but I've got time this afternoon.")
- Set a return-to-focus time ("I can meet now, but I'll resketch my content work to tomorrow.")
- Protect *tomorrow's* energy (don't stack extra work without making room for it)

You can be collaborative **and** clear. That's the Sketch Planner's secret sauce.

Clarity Creates Better Collaboration

When you know your Kings...

When you protect your blocks...

When you set expectations with kindness...

You're not *less available*—you're more effective.

Sketch Planning isn't about walling yourself off from your team.

It's about leading by example—with clear focus, consistent boundaries, and a rhythm that supports *you and everyone around you.*

Because your time is valuable.

Your energy is valuable.

And when you bring Sketch Planning into your work relationships?

You lift the whole team with you.

Reviewing and Refining Work Plans

Because the plan that worked last month might not work next week—and that's totally okay.

Let's get honest:

Even the most well-organized, beautifully color-coded Sketch Plan is going to need tweaking.

Not because you did something wrong.

Not because your schedule is a disaster.

But because **you're human. And so is your life.**

You're not a robot in a controlled lab setting.

You're juggling real responsibilities, shifting priorities, surprise client needs, changing family dynamics, and that one random week where everyone gets sick and the power goes out.

So instead of building a plan that stays perfect forever (which, let's be real, is a myth), Sketch Planning encourages you to **continually reflect and refine**—so your work plan grows *with* you, not against you.

Let's make that process feel natural, supportive, and even a little empowering.

Why Ongoing Review Matters (Especially for Women Balancing It All)

When we don't stop to review our plan, we:

- Keep repeating the same mistakes
- Overcommit without realizing it
- Misjudge our time, again and again
- Forget to acknowledge what's *actually working*

- Slide into autopilot—even when that autopilot is headed for burnout

You're not doing "too much."

You're just overdue for a reset.

Sketch Planning gives you the perfect structure to stop, zoom out, and say:

"What's helping me move forward? And what's just in the way?"

The Power of the Weekly Reset Ritual

Once a week (I love Fridays or Sunday nights), take 10–15 minutes to reflect on your work plan.

Do this with a journal, a digital doc, a scrap of paper, or even in your planner margins.

Try this 3-part reflection:

What worked well this week?
Finished 3 out of 4 work kings
Admin day was smooth
Loved batching tasks
What felt off or overloaded?
Afternoon blocks keep getting hijacked
Didn't leave buffer before big meeting
Forgot two things because they weren't sketched
What will I try differently next week?
Move creative work earlier in the day
Add a 30-min decompression block after calls
Add "day of" review at 8:30 am

This isn't a performance review—it's a *grace-filled check-in* with your goals, your energy, and your reality.

Common Signs Your Work Plan Needs Refining

You'll know it's time for a tune-up when:

- You keep skipping or rescheduling the same task
- Your Time Blocks feel rushed, disjointed, or way too ambitious
- Your Work Kings don't reflect your *current* priorities
- You end the day wondering, "What did I even accomplish?"

- You feel constant pressure—even though you have a plan

That's your cue to re-sketch. Not as a reset to zero, but as a **course correction**.

Zoom Out on Your Work Kings

It's easy to fall into "default mode" where we treat *everything* as urgent—or worse, keep doing tasks that made sense last month but no longer serve us.

Use your review time to ask:

- Are my current Work Kings aligned with my bigger goals?
- Do I actually need to be the one doing this—or could it be delegated or delayed?
- What new King(s) are emerging that deserve more space?

Every time I launch a product, I *think* I'll get back to evergreen work right after. But I've learned to give myself a full week after launch just to regroup, handle customer support, and clean up lingering admin stuff. That's a new Work King I've built into my post-launch rhythm.

Revisit Your Block Structure (Yes, Even the Ones You Love)

Even your favorite blocks might need adjusting when:

- Your energy shifts
- Your availability changes
- Your business goals evolve
- You're in a new season (summer, launch time, holidays, etc.)

For example:

- Your Morning Focus Block might shrink during school break

- You might need a weekly "CEO Time" block for vision work
- You may realize your creative work flows better after lunch (surprise!)
- Or maybe that 3–5pm block keeps getting hijacked by carpool or fatigue

Adjust the structure to match your *current capacity*—not the idealized version of yourself who somehow never gets tired and always has makeup on. (We love her, but she's not real.)

Reflect on Boundaries and Communication, Too

If your plan keeps getting interrupted or overwritten by someone else's needs (clients, coworkers, team members, kids, etc.), your review should include boundary questions:

- Did I communicate my availability clearly this week?
- Am I saying yes to too much?
- Where did I sacrifice deep work for quick wins—or guilt?
- Do I need to shift my meeting availability or reframe expectations?

Reviewing isn't just about logistics. It's about reclaiming your *ownership* of your work life.

Build the Habit of Tiny Adjustments

Refining doesn't have to mean reinventing. Most of the time, it's just one or two little tweaks that make a big difference:

- Swapping two tasks
- Reassigning a King to a different day

- Adding 15 minutes of margin before or after a call
- Moving a recurring task from Thursday to Tuesday because *Thursday is cursed* (you know the feeling)

Give yourself permission to experiment.

Sketch Planning = smart plans, softened by grace.

You're the Leader of Your Plan

Too many women are stuck in reaction mode—responding to demands, deadlines, and other people's urgency.

Reviewing and refining your plan regularly helps you shift back into *intentionality.*

It's how you:

- Stay aligned with your real goals
- Adjust your rhythm to your season
- Catch burnout before it hits
- And build a business, career, or creative life that actually fits your life

You don't need to do more.

You just need to make your *current effort* work smarter for you.

That's what Sketch Planning gives you.

And refining your plan isn't a redo—it's a sign you're growing.

8

Planning for Students: Mastering Academic Organization

Prioritizing Academic Tasks

Because straight A's don't mean much if you're surviving on caffeine, anxiety, and granola bars.

Ah, student life.

Whether you're the one in school or you're parenting someone who is, you know it's a whirlwind:

- Papers due by midnight
- Back-to-back group projects
- Study sessions that turn into memes and pizza
- Club meetings, practices, rehearsals

- Family obligations (yep, you still have to show up for those)
- And let's not forget trying to maintain some kind of social life and mental health

With all that on your plate, even the best planner can feel more like a guilt journal than a productivity tool.

But that's where Sketch Planning saves the day.

Because instead of trying to cram everything into rigid time slots or endlessly rewriting a to-do list that makes you want to cry, **you create a flexible, big-picture plan that works with your energy, schedule, and goals.**

Let's talk about how to make it happen—without losing your mind (or your GPA).

1: Identify Your Academic Kings

Just like in work and life, some school tasks *matter more than others.*

These are your **Academic Kings**—your non-negotiables.

They might be:

- An upcoming midterm or final
- A paper that's worth 40% of your grade
- Weekly readings or online quizzes that unlock other assignments
- A rehearsal or practice that's tied to a performance or competition
- A meeting with your advisor that affects your class schedule

Ask yourself:

"If I only got ONE academic thing done today (or this week), what would make the biggest impact?"

That's a King.

Put those Kings into your Time Blocks *before* you say yes to another club meeting or scroll through TikTok "just for a sec."

2: Sketch Your Week—With Everything On the Table

You can't plan for what you don't see.

So start each week by **laying out the whole picture**:

- Class schedule (fixed)
- Due dates (pull from syllabi or assignment portals)
- Study sessions
- Work shifts (if you've got a job)
- Sports, clubs, lessons, etc.
- Family responsibilities
- *Actual downtime* (yes, this goes on the plan too!)

Use a weekly overview format where each day includes 2–3 blocks max. Avoid overplanning with micro-tasks. Instead, focus on **theme blocks** like:

- "Study Block"
- "Essay Work Block"
- "Lab/Science Block"
- "Rest & Reset Block"
- "Catch-Up / Overflow Block"

My note for moms supporting students:

Help your kid sketch their week on Sunday. Let them do the writing—you just ask questions like, *"When will you prep for that history test?"* or *"What block is for catching up if Monday's math takes longer?"*

They learn time awareness *and* get confidence knowing they're in control of their week.

3: Balance Academic Goals with Life (Seriously.)

It's easy to get caught in the "just one more thing" spiral when you're a student.

But here's what happens when you overfill your sketch:

- You burn out faster
- You stop enjoying school
- You procrastinate (because your list is too long)
- You feel guilty for doing literally anything fun

That's not how you win at school—or life.

So be honest:

- Do you have at least 1 block each day where your brain can rest?
- Are you leaving margin between study blocks and extracurriculars?
- Did you sketch time to eat? Shower? Breathe?
- Are you giving yourself credit for showing up consistently—even if not perfectly?

Sketch Planning works *because it gives you permission to slow down when needed.*

4: Break Assignments Into Mini Kings

Big tasks need small, sketchable steps.

Instead of "write essay," try:

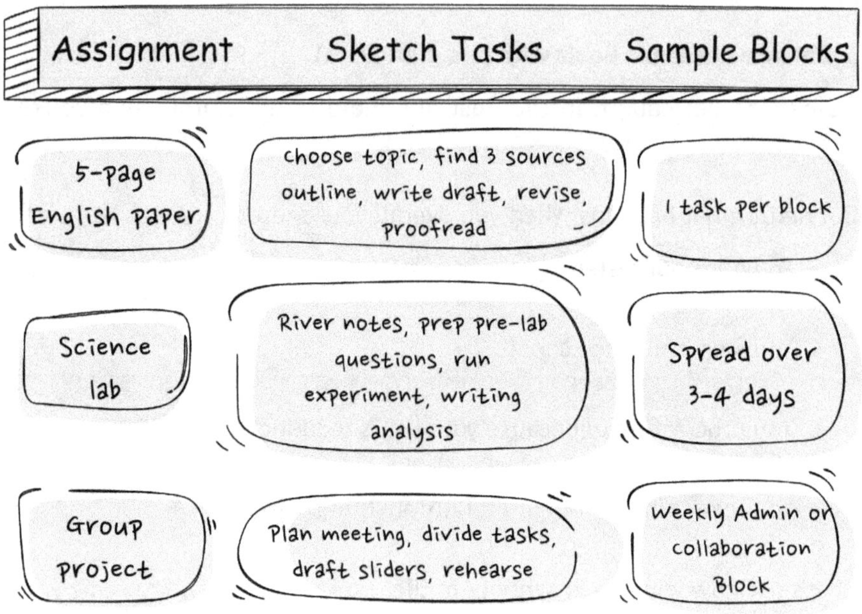
Assignment
Sketch Tasks
Sample Blocks
5-page English paper
choose topic, find 3 sources outline, write draft, revise, proofread
1 task per block
Science lab
River notes, prep pre-lab questions, run experiment, writing analysis
Spread over 3-4 days
Group project
Plan meeting, divide tasks, draft sliders, rehearse
weekly Admin or collaboration Block

This turns mountains into molehills—and makes you far more likely to finish early instead of cramming the night before.

5: Manage the Distraction Monsters

Let's be honest:

Half the battle isn't the task—it's staying focused long enough to start or finish it.

Here are some anti-distraction Sketch Hacks:

- **Pomodoro timer:** 25 minutes on, 5 off

- **Body doubling:** Study with a friend (in person or via Zoom)
- **Tech blockers:** Use Forest, Cold Turkey, or Freedom
- **Reward system:** Block time to scroll, watch, or game *after* you complete a Focus Block
- **Use "I'm in a block" signals:** Headphones, sticky notes, a closed door—even if it's symbolic

It's not about discipline. It's about reducing resistance.

Bonus: Schedule Wins and Rewards

Let's normalize celebrating effort—not just perfect grades.

When you finish a big assignment? Sketch a block for your favorite show

Schedule a night with friends

Block out an hour to *do nothing*

Treat yourself to a coffee or boba

Small rewards create *big momentum*—and make planning something you look forward to, not something you resent.

You're the Architect of Your Academic Success

No one else is going to organize your week, remind you to rest, or make sure you're not melting down over back-to-back deadlines.

But *you* can.

Sketch Planning puts you in the driver's seat of your school life.

It helps you show up prepared, make space for your real life, and still reach your goals—without breaking down in the process.

Whether you're learning to manage your own schedule or supporting a student who is—this method brings structure without suffocation.

You've got this.

And now you've got a way to *plan smarter*—not harder.

Managing Study Time

Because "I studied all day" isn't helpful if you can't remember any of it tomorrow.

Studying. It's the thing we know we *should* be doing, but somehow it ends up meaning:

- Staring blankly at a screen
- Opening the book but rereading the same paragraph five times
- Pretending to "review notes" while scrolling Instagram
- Cramming four hours of material into 45 minutes the night before the test

And then we wonder why it doesn't stick.

The truth is, most people have never been taught *how* to study effectively.

They were just told, "Try harder" or "Make flashcards."

But with Sketch Planning, you don't just make time to study—you make it *count.*

Let's talk about how to turn those Time Blocks into focused, productive sessions—without overwhelm, guilt, or brain fog.

1: Know What Type of Study You're Doing

This might sound obvious, but many students (and adults!) just block out "Study time" and hope for the best.

But **not all studying is the same**, and if you don't match your method to the material, you'll end up wasting time.

Break it into categories:

Type of Task	Best Block Approach
Memorization (vocab, facts, dates)	Short bursts with repetition & recall
comprehension (textbook reading, articles)	High-focus block, minimal distractions
Application (math, coding, problem-solving)	Practice problems during focused block
creation (writhing essays, building projects)	Longer blocks with minimal interruptions
collaboration (group work, tutoring, review sessions)	Midday or social-energy block

My real-life example:

When my daughter has vocab quizzes, we block 20-minute study sprints three times throughout the day instead of one long session. She remembers *way more*, and it doesn't feel like a chore.

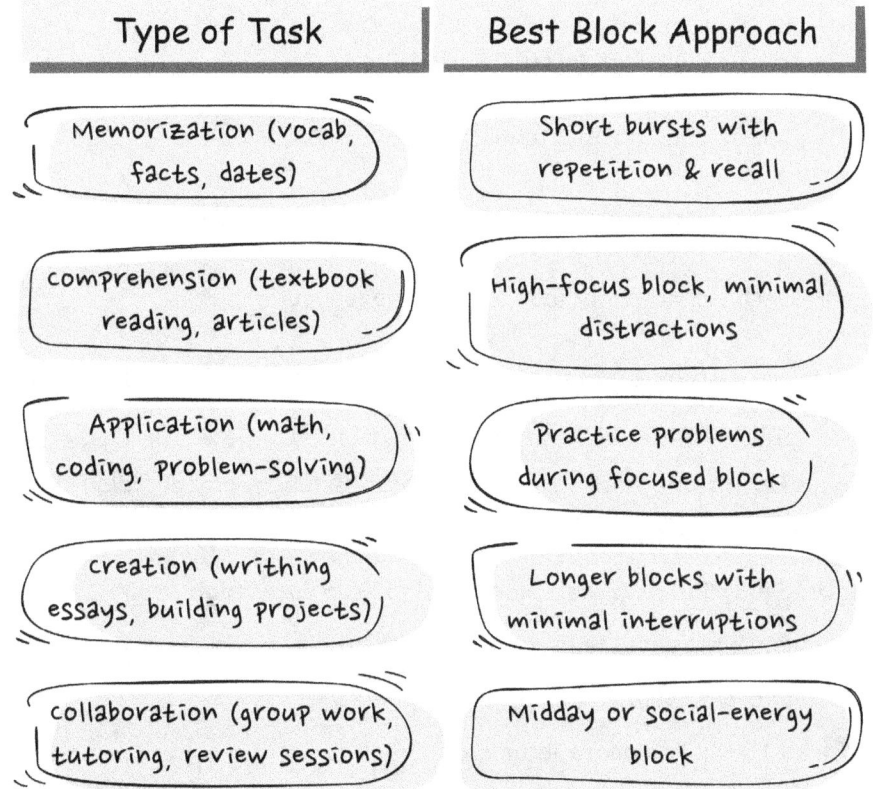

2: Break Big Goals into Small, Sketchable Wins

"I need to study biology" is not helpful. It's vague and overwhelming.

Instead, ask:

"What specifically do I need to learn or practice today?"

Then sketch it like this:

- Review Chapter 5 summary
- Watch one lecture recording
- Quiz self on 10 vocab terms
- Do 5 practice questions
- Teach a concept out loud to someone (or your dog)

When your study tasks are **small and specific**, your Time Blocks feel doable—and you're way more likely to start *and* finish.

Bonus Tip: If a study session feels heavy or stressful, you probably didn't break it down far enough.

3: Use Study Sprints (a.k.a. Pomodoros) to Keep Focus High

Your brain wasn't built to focus for hours at a time—especially when it's tired, anxious, or overstimulated (hello, modern life).

Instead, try the **Pomodoro Technique**:

1. Study for 25 minutes (no distractions!)
2. Take a 5-minute break
3. Repeat 3–4 times
4. Then take a longer 15–30 minute break

This gives your brain a *rhythm* to follow, and it lowers resistance to starting.

Use this sketch layout:

Evening Study Block (6:00–7:30 p.m.)

Pomodoro 1: Flashcards – Science vocab

Pomodoro 2: Practice quiz

Short break – water + stretch

Pomodoro 3: Review wrong answers

Reward block: 30-min Netflix episode

It doesn't have to be intense to be effective.

4: Remove Study Sabotagers Before You Start

We all have them:

- Your phone lighting up with notifications
- Tabs open to 15 different unrelated things
- That sudden urge to reorganize your desk or bake cookies
- "Let me check this one thing real quick..." (famous last words)

Before your block begins:

- Turn on Do Not Disturb
- Close all non-study tabs
- Put your phone in another room (or app lock it)
- Grab water, snacks, a hoodie—whatever you need to stay seated
- Tell others you're in a "focus block" and not available (yes, even roommates or partners)

If you're supporting a student, set the environment up for success. Let them know *you've got their back* and will help protect that focus time.

5: Actively Engage with What You're Learning

Passive studying (rereading, highlighting, skimming notes) is like *watching someone else work out and hoping you get stronger.*

Active studying means doing something with the material:

- Write your own summary
- Teach it to someone
- Quiz yourself without looking
- Create diagrams, mind maps, or silly mnemonics
- Say it out loud, draw it, or explain it from memory

Sketch Block Example:

"Afternoon Study (2:00–3:00)"

Watch 10-min YouTube video on mitosis

Pause and take notes

Draw process by hand

Explain to my little sister in 30 seconds (bonus points if she laughs)

Fun, weird, memorable = your brain retains it.

6: Know When to Study Alone vs. with Others

Sometimes you need silence and focus.

Sometimes you need accountability or group input.

If you're:

- Distracted easily

- Falling behind
- Not starting at all

...then it might be time to call in a friend, join a study group, or even just have a body-double session (you both work silently on Zoom or at a table).

Sketch Planning with others:

Try adding shared Study Blocks with a buddy:

- "Tuesday 7–9: Study call with Jess – Quiz review"
- "Saturday 10–12: Coffee shop study with Emily – Final prep"

Planning it ahead keeps it intentional—not chaotic.

7: Use Flex Blocks to Review or Catch Up

Didn't finish what you planned today? No worries.

Flex Blocks are there to:

- Finish what got pushed
- Review material before a test
- Wrap up something that ran long
- Rebalance your week after a busy day

Sketch Planning is about *momentum*, not perfection. You're still winning—even if you move things around.

My Tip:

Teach your student (or remind yourself) that *resketching isn't quitting—it's adjusting*. That's the power of the plan. You stay in control.

Study Time Should Serve *You*

Studying doesn't have to feel like punishment.

It doesn't have to be perfect.

And it doesn't have to take over your life.

With Sketch Planning, your study sessions become:

- Clear
- Focused
- Realistic
- And actually effective

You don't need to do *more*—you just need to study *smarter*.

So go ahead—sketch your next Study Block.

Make it short. Make it focused. Make it yours.

You've got this. And now you've got a system that has your back.

Handling Academic Deadlines

Because "I'll do it later" is a lie we've all believed—and it never ends well.

Deadlines have a special kind of power.

They loom. They whisper guilt. They sneak up on you like a ninja in a hoodie.

And if you're juggling multiple classes, extracurriculars, and a social life (or you're the mom of a student who is), those deadlines can pile up fast.

We've all had the *"I totally forgot that was due today!"* moment. Or the *"I had three weeks to do this and started it the night before"* meltdown.

But here's the good news:

Sketch Planning can help you avoid deadline panic, keep your brain calm, and *still* leave room for Netflix and snacks.

Let's break it down.

1: Gather All the Deadlines (Like, All of Them)

First things first: you can't plan for what you haven't seen.

So before the semester really gets rolling, set aside one power hour to gather **every single due date** from:

- Syllabi
- Assignment portals
- Group projects
- Club events
- Scholarship or internship apps
- Anything else school-related that has a time limit

Tip: Use a monthly calendar view (paper or digital) to log them. Color-code them if that helps you visualize the chaos.

Now? You've got the whole mountain in front of you—no more getting blindsided.

2: Work Backwards from the Deadline (AKA "Future You" Will Thank You)

This is where most people mess up:

They sketch the deadline, but forget to plan for the *work leading up to it.*

So instead of sketching:

"History paper - Due Friday"

Try this instead:

- Monday: Choose topic & outline
- Tuesday: Draft intro + 1 body paragraph
- Wednesday: Finish draft
- Thursday: Edit + format citations
- Friday: Submit

When you work backwards, you eliminate the *cram-and-cry* cycle.

When I was in school (and honestly, sometimes even now), I used to block the due date and think that was enough. Spoiler: it wasn't. Now I reverse-engineer every major task into mini-Kings so I'm never relying on a last-minute miracle.

3: Break It Into Sketchable Tasks

Your Time Blocks aren't built for vague tasks like "Work on essay."

They're built for **clear, doable steps**.

Use verbs and outcomes like:

- "Write outline for essay"
- "Answer 5 review questions"
- "Record voice memo explaining Chapter 3"
- "Meet with group to divide project tasks"
- "Submit final doc to portal by 9 PM"

Each one goes into a specific Time Block, just like a Work King would.

When you can picture exactly what you're doing in the block? You're way more likely to *actually do it.*

4: Use the 48-Hour Safety Rule

Here's a rule that'll save you from late-night panic:

Plan to finish every major task at least 48 hours before it's due.

Why? Because life happens:

- You get sick
- Wi-Fi goes down
- A surprise test pops up
- You misread the assignment (oops)
- Your printer dies (RIP)

Building in a 2-day buffer means you can *breathe*, make edits, or troubleshoot without the stress-induced meltdown.

Bonus: That 48-hour space also lets you ask for help before it's too late.

5: Track Deadlines Visually—So They Stick in Your Brain

Having deadlines written in four different places? Not helpful.

Try one (or more) of these:

- A monthly calendar overview with big dates
- A weekly planner where you list that week's priority deadlines
- Sticky notes on your wall or whiteboard
- A digital dashboard or calendar reminder
- A "Countdown Corner" in your notebook (5 days till essay, 3 till project...)

When your brain sees it often, it stops being a surprise—and starts being something you *plan for on purpose.*

6: Use Flex Blocks for Overflow or Catch-Up

Despite your best efforts, sometimes the research takes longer, or your focus disappears mid-block.

That's why your Sketch Plan includes **Flex Blocks**—little buffer zones where you can:

- Finish what got bumped
- Tidy up before submitting
- Add polish or review details
- Just *breathe* before hitting send

Instead of working right up to the wire, your deadline becomes just one more task in a well-paced week.

7: For Group Projects—Sketch It AND Share It

Ah, group projects. Where three people do the work and one person never replies to the group chat.

Don't leave it up to fate.

Sketch Planning for group work includes:

- Setting shared mini-deadlines (not just the final one)
- Assigning tasks to specific people
- Scheduling at least one "pull-it-all-together" session 2–3 days before it's due
- Writing a backup plan for things that might go wrong (like your part-

ner's laptop "accidentally" crashing the night before)

If possible, share your sketch or timeline with your group—because structure helps *everyone*, not just you.

8: Review Your Deadline Patterns Every Week

Each week, ask:

- What deadlines are coming up in the next 7–10 days?
- What tasks do I need to break down?
- What can I sketch now so I'm not panicking later?
- Did anything take longer than expected last week—and do I need more prep time next time?

This makes your Sketch Plan *smarter* over time.

Deadlines Don't Have to Be Stress Triggers

They can be motivators, mile markers, and even *confidence boosters*—if you plan for them well.

You don't need to cram.

You don't need to guess.

And you definitely don't need to hate your calendar.

With Sketch Planning, deadlines become just another part of your week—not the boss of it.

So take a breath.

Pull out your calendar.

Break it down.

Sketch it in.

And get it done—with time to spare.

Participating in Extracurriculars

Because being "well-rounded" shouldn't leave you flat-out exhausted.

Extracurriculars can be amazing.

They build confidence, friendships, leadership, creativity, and college apps that don't scream "I only studied and cried."

They give kids and teens (and, let's be real, a lot of adults too) a place to express who they really are outside the classroom.

But...

They also take time. A lot of time.

And if they aren't planned for properly, they can take over—leaving no space for homework, sleep, or sanity.

Sketch Planning helps you manage extracurriculars in a way that keeps life balanced.

You can stay involved without sacrificing your mental health, academic goals, or a basic human need like dinner.

1: Define Your "Activity Kings"

Just like schoolwork has Academic Kings, extracurriculars have their own non-negotiables.

Ask:

"What activities happen every week, no matter what?"

These could be:

- Soccer practices

- Club meetings
- Rehearsals
- Church youth group
- Part-time work
- Student council
- Volunteer shifts

These are your **Activity Kings**—they get scheduled first.

You wouldn't plan a study session at the same time as your rehearsal, right? So don't accidentally sketch your to-dos without first making space for these recurring events.

Pro Tip for Parents:

If your child is managing multiple extracurriculars, sit down together each Sunday to list the week's Activity Kings first. It's a great way to help them learn time ownership while avoiding meltdowns on Wednesday night.

2: Map Out Your Week—Honestly

Here's where it gets real: extracurriculars aren't just about the meeting or the game.

There's prep time.

There's travel.

There's decompression after.

And sometimes there's "Oh no, I forgot my gear and now everything's chaos."

So when you sketch your schedule:

- **Add 15–30 minutes before and after each event**

- Be honest about how tired or energized you'll feel after
- Block time for eating and resting (seriously, this gets skipped too often)

Sample sketch:

Now your evening feels *doable*, not like you're trying to do math with wet hair and an empty stomach.

3: Balance Fun and Function—So You Don't Burn Out

Let's talk about burnout.

Just because an activity is fun or valuable doesn't mean your schedule can hold *all of them at once.*

Sketch Planning gives you visibility so you can ask:

- "Do I have space this week to fully enjoy this activity?"
- "What's getting pushed out of my week to make room for this?"
- "Is there time for rest if I say yes to this new commitment?"

Signs of extracurricular overload:

- You're staying up late *every* night to finish homework
- You stop looking forward to activities you used to enjoy
- You keep saying "yes" out of obligation, not excitement
- Your weekends disappear under a pile of uniforms, sheet music, and to-do lists

Reminder: Your Time Blocks don't lie.

If the sketch doesn't fit, the schedule doesn't either.

4: Use Time Blocks to Make Space for School (Even When Life Is Full)

This one's for every student who's said:

"I'll just do it after practice."

Spoiler: After practice is usually when your brain wants snacks, not Shakespeare.

Instead of leaving homework to fate, **use Time Blocks to plan smart around your activities.**

See how it fits?

No rushing. No skipping. No meltdown at 9:00 p.m.

We treat practices and rehearsals like any other King in our house. We sketch around them—not over them—so we still get things done without anyone turning into a stressed-out gremlin.

5: Create Boundaries Around New Commitments

This one's for the joiners. The achievers. The over-volunteers.

It's *very* easy to say yes to one more thing:

- One more club
- One more fundraiser
- One more volunteer shift
- One more "quick" group meeting

Sketch Planning acts as a **truth-teller**.

Before you say yes, ask:

- "Where does this actually fit in my sketch?"
- "What will I have to move or drop to make room?"
- "Is this something I *want* to do—or just something I *feel bad* saying no

to?”

You’re not being selfish when you say no.

You’re being wise with your energy.

6: Communicate With the Adults in the Room

If you're overwhelmed, **talk to someone**:

- Tell your coach when you need a breather
- Ask your club leader if you can scale back for a week
- Let your parents know you’re maxed out
- Ask your teacher for a lighter week if you’re juggling major events

Sketch Planning helps you *see* conflicts before they spiral, so you can advocate for yourself early and calmly.

If you're the parent:

Encourage your kid to name where their time is going. Help them draft a message to a coach or teacher if they’re unsure how to set a boundary. It builds lifelong self-advocacy skills.

7: Use Weekly Reviews to Make Tweaks

At the end of each week (or before the new one starts), do a check-in:

What activities felt life-giving this week?

What felt draining or frustrating?

What needs adjusting for next week’s energy level?

Maybe you skip one meeting.

Maybe you swap a late-night study session for an early morning one.

Maybe you simply sketch **more margin** around your busiest days.

This is the Sketch Planning magic—it *evolves* with your week, your needs, and your season.

You Don't Have to Be Everything to Everyone

You can be involved.

You can show up.

You can lead, perform, play, serve, or cheer with your whole heart.

But you don't have to do it all at once.

And you definitely don't have to sacrifice your mental health, your rest, or your joy in the process.

Sketch Planning helps you see your week clearly, so you can choose the right mix of "yes," "not right now," and "maybe later."

You're still amazing even when you do less.

So go on. Sketch your week. Make room for what matters. And give yourself permission to drop the rest.

Reviewing and Adjusting Academic Plans

Because what worked last week might not work this week—and that's totally normal.

Academic life is anything but static.

One week you feel on top of it all:

All assignments turned in

Study sessions flowing

Notes organized

Even time for a Netflix episode or two

The next week?

A pop quiz, a late-night rehearsal, an unexpected group project, and boom—your beautiful plan goes off the rails.

Sketch Planning is built for this.

It's not meant to be perfect. It's meant to be *flexible*.

And part of that flexibility comes from regularly stepping back and asking:

"How's this actually working for me right now?"

This chapter is all about how to *check in, adjust, and reset* so academic success stays within reach—even when life throws you curveballs.

1: Set a Weekly Academic Review Ritual

Make it a habit to look back before you sketch forward.

Pick a regular time—Friday afternoon, Sunday evening, or even Monday morning—and walk through a quick review of the past week.

Try this simple 3-question reflection:

What went well?

"I finished my research paper early!"

"I actually remembered that vocab quiz—thanks, study block."

What felt off or stressful?

"I didn't leave enough time for science reading."

"That club meeting totally cut into my study time."

What can I do differently next week?

"Start group project earlier."

"Move heavy reading to mornings when my brain is fresh."

You don't need a spreadsheet or fancy journal—just consistent awareness.

2: Adjust Your Time Blocks Based on Energy and Reality

You might *want* to study every day at 8 p.m.

But if your brain checks out after dinner? That block's not working.

Use your review to identify patterns like:

- Always bumping the same type of assignment
- Repeatedly cramming at the last minute
- Running out of time after extracurriculars
- Forgetting small tasks like readings or group prep

Then adjust:

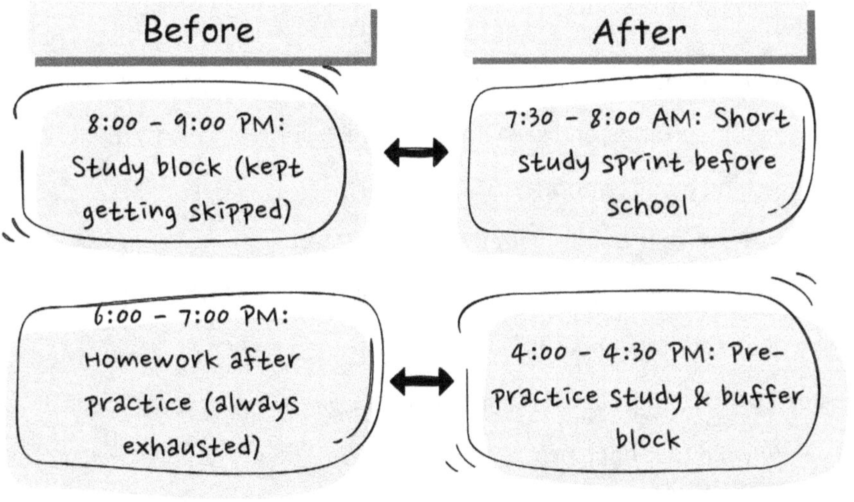

It's not about changing everything—it's about *changing the right things.*

3: Update Academic Priorities As They Shift

Each week, your school life shifts slightly:

- New units start
- Projects become more urgent

- Some subjects get harder
- Others (thankfully) get easier

Your Academic Kings will change—and your plan should too.

Ask:

- What subject needs more attention this week?
- What can move to maintenance mode for now?
- Are any new deadlines creeping up?

Sketch Planning helps you respond quickly without overhauling your whole schedule.

When my daughter hits a week with multiple tests, we shift her sketch to focus on test prep Kings, and save lighter subjects for review-only mode. It's all about matching focus to priority.

4: Learn From Your Bumps (Not Beat Yourself Up)

Did you miss a study session? Turn in something late? Bomb a quiz?

Okay. Cool. Let's talk about it.

Instead of spiraling, Sketch Planning invites you to ask:

- *Why* did that happen?
- Was the task too big or vague?
- Was the time block poorly placed?
- Were you overscheduled?
- Did you just need rest?

Mistakes are data. Not character flaws.

Use that data to plan better next time—and move forward.

5: Communicate With Teachers, Parents, or Classmates

If your plan consistently isn't working, don't keep it to yourself.

Your review might reveal you need to:

- Ask a teacher for an extension
- Shift your role in a group project
- Tell a parent you're overbooked
- Request help setting boundaries with your time

Sketch Planning gives you the clarity to advocate for yourself—**with confidence and clarity**.

Bonus: Use a Weekly Planner Snapshot

Try this once a week:

1. Circle next week's **Academic Kings**
2. Highlight any extracurricular conflicts
3. Identify which blocks are too tight or unrealistic
4. Pick one block to loosen up or protect for rest
5. Write down one thing you're doing *really well*

This 5-minute reset helps your next week feel like a fresh start—not a runaway train.

Adjusting Isn't Quitting—It's Mastering

You don't have to stick to a plan that's no longer serving you.

You don't have to "push through" a rhythm that's making you miserable.

You're allowed to reset.

You're encouraged to reflect.

You're empowered to create a schedule that supports your learning *and* your life.

Because real success in school doesn't come from a flawless plan.

It comes from a flexible one.

One that moves with you—not against you.

And now you've got the tools to make that happen.

9

Planning for Families: Achieving Harmony and Efficiency

Prioritizing Family Responsibilities

Because being the glue that holds it all together shouldn't mean feeling like you're constantly coming unglued.

If you're a mom, chances are high that your brain is doing about 67 things at once at any given moment.

You're:

- Answering a client email while sneaking in a bathroom break
- Mentally adding "buy toilet paper" to your list during a Zoom call
- Reminding yourself (again) that tomorrow is library book day
- Wondering if that weird noise in the laundry room means a sock is about

to cause a plumbing emergency

- Planning dinner based on what's defrosted and whether anyone will actually eat it

You're managing the calendar, the house, the health stuff, the emotional stuff, the snack stuff, the school stuff, the everything.

And you're tired. Because no planner in the world seems to **actually help manage the kind of flexible chaos you live in every day**.

That's where **Sketch Planning** comes in.

This isn't about creating a picture-perfect life.

It's about **making room for your actual one**—the messy, beautiful, loud, unpredictable one you're living.

Let's talk about how to balance the many roles you carry without constantly feeling like something's falling through the cracks.

1: Identify Your "Family Kings" (Yes, Some Kid Stuff is a Non-Negotiable)

The first to balancing family life is **naming what truly matters every week**—and not everything counts.

Family Kings are your non-negotiables, the things that MUST happen to keep life functional and semi-peaceful.

These might include:

- School drop-off and pick-up
- Meal prep (or at least dinner on the table)
- Homework help
- Bedtime routines

- Appointments (pediatrician, dentist, vet—oh my)
- One-on-one time with your kids or partner
- Grocery shopping or restocking the pantry before everyone revolts

These go into your Time Blocks **first**—before you sketch work, errands, or anything else.

On school days, I always block out 7:15–7:45 a.m. for the school run. That's a Family King. It doesn't change. It's not up for debate. And by sketching it in first, I'm not scrambling to rearrange my workday every morning—it's already accounted for.

2: Treat Family Logistics Like a Job—Because It *Is* One

You don't have to prove that household management is "real work." It's running a *tiny corporation of humans* with very strong snack preferences and zero chill about missing Pajama Day.

So give it the respect it deserves:

- Sketch a **Home Admin Block** once or twice a week
- Use it to meal plan, check calendars, pay bills, fill out school forms, schedule appointments, etc.
- Light a candle and play music so it feels *slightly less like soul erosion*

Instead of feeling like these things are constantly creeping into your brain all day long, you give them a home. One place. One time.

My real-life Tip:

Thursday mornings are my "household CEO block." It's when I tackle all the stuff that keeps the house running: order groceries, update school calendar, plan next week's dinners, clean out the bottom of my purse, check the dog's food supply—you get the idea. If it lives in the background noise of my brain, it gets handled during that time.

3: Build Your Week Around Rhythms—Not Rigid Schedules

Rigid hourly schedules will fail you every time.

Someone will get sick.

The dog will eat something weird.

Your 3 p.m. meeting will run long, and your dinner will burn because you were trying to multitask like a ninja.

Instead, **Sketch Planning uses Time Blocks**—chunky periods of time (2–4 hours) built around energy and rhythm, not minute-by-minute perfection.

Your family has natural rhythms:

- Mornings are usually busy and chaotic (don't expect deep work then)
- Afternoons may require pickups, snack service, or emotional regulation
- Evenings are for winding down and prepping for tomorrow
- Weekends often get swallowed by events, activities, or rest catch-up

So sketch accordingly.

Sample Sketch Plan (School Day)

- 6:00–8:30 AM: Family Block (get ready, breakfast, drop-off)
- 9:00–12:00 PM: Work King Block (deep work while house is quiet)
- 12:00–1:00 PM: Flex/Admin (lunch, errands, calls)
- 1:00–3:00 PM: Work King #2

- 3:00–5:00 PM: Family Block (pickup, snacks, decompress)
- 5:00–7:00 PM: Dinner + Reset Block
- 7:00–9:00 PM: Personal Block or overflow

4: Use Theme Days to Stay Grounded

Theme days are a Sketch Planning power move.

Here's how they work:

- **Monday:** Household Admin Day
- **Tuesday:** Client Work + Calls
- **Wednesday:** Project Block
- **Thursday:** Family Focus (appointments, errands)
- **Friday:** Catch-up + Creative
- **Saturday:** Fun + Flex
- **Sunday:** Reset + Sketch the Week

You're not chaining yourself to a schedule—you're giving your brain anchors.

When everything feels messy, your themes help you remember:

"This is the day I handle that."

5: Make Space for YOU—Without Apologizing for It

This one is big. Like, life-changing big.

Because I know what it feels like to *always* be on. To think:

- "I'll rest when everything else is done."
- "I can't take a break—there's too much to do."

- "If I stop for a second, it'll all fall apart."

But you matter. Your well-being matters. And **you can't pour from an empty cup**—no matter how color-coded your planner is.

So sketch your Personal Kings:

- A 20-minute walk after school drop-off
- Reading for 15 minutes at night
- Taking yourself for a coffee
- Watching your show without folding laundry at the same time
- Sitting in your car in silence for 10 minutes before walking inside (this counts!!)

You don't need a spa day to reset. You just need *space that's yours.*

And when it's sketched in? It becomes *just as important* as grocery shopping or that Zoom call.

6: Talk About the Plan with Your People

You are not the only one in this household with a brain (even if it feels like it sometimes).

- Post the family's week on a whiteboard, fridge, or app
- Have a 10-minute "family huddle" on Sunday nights
- Let your partner know when your blocks are protected
- Teach your kids the language of Time Blocks (it's life-changing for them too!)

This builds awareness and ownership. It stops the revolving door of "Hey, what's the plan?" questions... and starts building *teamwork* instead.

7: Adjust As You Go—Without Guilt

You will miss things.

Plans will get hijacked.

Kids will get fevers.

Dinner will be cereal.

That's life.

The beauty of Sketch Planning is that it bends with you. You can **resketch your day, move your Kings, shift blocks**, and still stay on track.

Flexibility isn't failure.

It's what makes this whole system *sustainable.*

You're Doing More Than You Realize

You're not lazy.

You're not behind.

You're not disorganized.

You're a woman carrying a lot—with heart, effort, and probably a little caffeine. You don't need a whole new personality to get it together. You just need a system that works with your life, not against it.

Sketch Planning is how you do that.

It brings order to your week, clarity to your mind, and space to be the mom, partner, worker, and *person* you want to be.

You're not meant to do it all.

You're meant to do what matters—on purpose.

And now you've got a way to do exactly that.

Managing Household Chores

Because your full-time job isn't scrubbing behind the toilet—and the house won't fall apart if the towels aren't folded like a department store display.

Let's be honest: household chores don't stop.

They don't even slow down.

They just kind of multiply in corners and sneak up on you while you're trying to live your life.

You wipe down the counters... then someone makes toast.

You finish the laundry... then realize there's a wet towel under the bed.

You vacuum... and two seconds later the dog walks through with muddy paws like he owns the place.

The problem isn't that you're doing it wrong.

The problem is that you're trying to do it *all*—often silently, constantly, and invisibly.

And I'm here to tell you: **it doesn't have to be this way.**

Sketch Planning gives you a way to **see what actually needs doing, create a doable rhythm, and share the load**—so the house is livable, and you're not constantly on edge wondering when the dishwasher fairy is going to show up. (Spoiler: she's not.)

Let's make home care feel *manageable, not maddening.*

First, Let's Name the Mental Load

One of the hardest parts of chores isn't doing them—it's keeping track of them.

There's the visible stuff (like dishes in the sink), and then there's the invisible layer:

- Noticing when something's running low
- Remembering that the trash needs to go out before pickup
- Realizing the dog needs a bath
- Knowing where the extra toilet paper is
- Keeping the paper clutter from turning into a stress pile on the counter

That's called the **mental load**, and if you're the default parent, odds are you're carrying it.

Sketch Planning helps get that swirl of responsibilities *out of your head and onto paper*—so you're not trying to remember it all at 10:45 p.m. when you're supposed to be asleep.

Start by creating a **household task brain dump**:

- Go room by room
- Write down everything that happens weekly (or should happen weekly, let's be honest)
- Include one-off tasks like "switch seasonal clothes" or "deep clean the fridge"

You'll quickly see: this isn't a short list.

Which means you shouldn't be the only one doing it.

Divide and Sketch: Creating Weekly Chore Blocks

Now that you've brain dumped the chores, don't just let them float around.

Sketch them into your Time Blocks, just like you would any King or work task.

There are a few different ways to do this:

1. Daily Mini Chore Blocks

Do 15–30 minutes per day, attached to another anchor activity (like after breakfast or before dinner).

Examples:

- Monday: Kitchen wipe-down + trash
- Tuesday: Bathrooms
- Wednesday: Laundry + dusting
- Thursday: Meal planning + fridge cleanout
- Friday: Floors
- Saturday: Catch-up or outside chores

This works really well if you like smaller chunks and fewer "big clean" days.

2. One Weekly Power Clean

Pick one 1–2 hour block each week and knock out everything at once.

This is great if you like momentum and want it done in one swoop.

I like a hybrid. I'll sketch 20–30 minute blocks throughout the week (like Monday morning for bathrooms, Thursday for floors), and then I keep Saturday mornings open as a Flex Block for anything I skipped. That way, if the week goes sideways (which it always does), I have a built-in backup.

Now Let's Talk Delegation (AKA: You Are Not the Only One With Hands)

Repeat after me:

"Just because I've always done it doesn't mean I always should."

Delegating chores is not about being bossy. It's about being wise. You're part of a household—not running a hotel. The people who live in the home should contribute to its care.

Depending on your family structure, delegation could look like:

- A partner owning specific categories (like garbage, dishes, or pet care)
- Kids having age-appropriate responsibilities
- Creating a shared "chore board" or rotating system
- Assigning weekend cleanup zones
- Outsourcing certain tasks (if it fits your budget) to free up time and sanity

Pro Tip: Pick one or two areas where you're most overburdened and hand those off first. Start small and consistent. Even if it's "your job is to clear the table every night," that's one less thing on your list.

And no, it won't be done *exactly like you would do it.*

That's okay. Done-ish is better than martyrdom.

Chores + Kids: Teaching, Not Just Tasking

If you've got kids, chores aren't just about helping out—they're about teaching life skills.

Yes, it takes longer at first.

Yes, they will complain.

Yes, they will do it halfway at best for a while.

But if you can stick with it, you're raising humans who know how to:

- Load a dishwasher

- Fold laundry
- Clean a bathroom
- Cook basic meals
- Manage their own space someday

Start with simple routines:

- 5-minute toy cleanup after dinner
- "Clean-up song" for little ones
- Teenagers own their own laundry basket
- Saturday morning zone cleaning with music

Make it visual if needed—a whiteboard, a printed checklist, a weekly sketch. They'll learn how to plan *and* clean, and you'll slowly out of the constant role of "default cleaner-upper."

The Weekly Chore Reset

Once a week, spend 5–10 minutes looking at the week ahead:

- What needs to be cleaned or handled?
- What was skipped last week and needs catch-up?
- What's feeling out of control (fridge, laundry, bedrooms)?
- What can you **skip** this week without guilt?

Sketch it in based on:

- Your family rhythm

- Who's home when
- Your energy levels
- Your bandwidth (hello, seasonal chaos)

When you look at the week holistically, it's easier to decide what's *essential* and what can wait.

Remember, cleanliness is subjective. You're aiming for functional, not perfection.

Clean Enough Is Clean Enough

There's always more that could be done.

Always more dust, more laundry, more clutter to sort, more things to put in bins with cute labels.

But here's the truth: you are allowed to stop when the house is **livable**, not perfect.

Sketch Planning helps you prioritize the chores that matter most *right now*—and let go of the ones that don't.

Because a clean house means nothing if it costs you your peace.

And trust me: your family would rather have a relaxed, happy mom in a slightly messy home... than a stressed-out, resentful one in a spotless one.

You're doing more than enough.

Now go sketch it in a way that proves it.

Planning Family Activities

Because your calendar shouldn't be all carpool, deadlines, and dentist appointments.

Here's something we forget way too often:

Fun is not a reward you earn.

Fun is part of what makes life sustainable.

And yet... when life gets busy (read: always), family fun becomes the first thing to get shoved off the sketch. Why? Because it feels optional. Or exhausting. Or like one more thing that takes energy you don't feel like you have.

But here's what I've learned:

If you don't plan for it, it doesn't happen.

And if it doesn't happen, the people in your house start to operate more like a task force than a family.

Sketch Planning isn't just about organizing your time—it's about making space for the things that make life *good.* That includes the messy game nights, the movie marathons, the random ice cream runs, and the "remember when..." moments that stick long after the chores are done.

Let's talk about how to plan fun on purpose, without making it feel like another thing to check off.

First: Redefine What "Family Fun" Means

A lot of us picture family fun like:

- A weekend road trip with zero fighting
- Everyone smiling in coordinated outfits at the apple orchard
- A four-course meal where the kids say "Wow, thanks, Mom!"

Yeah... no.

Family fun doesn't have to be fancy, photogenic, or wildly creative. It just has to be **intentional**.

Fun can be:

- Playing a silly game before bedtime
- Ordering takeout and eating on a blanket in the living room
- Doing a puzzle while watching a show
- Taking a walk and seeing who can spot the most squirrels
- Making popcorn and watching an old movie together
- Listening to music while cleaning the house and having a spontaneous dance break

It's not about big. It's about **shared experiences**—the little things that help your people feel seen, safe, and connected.

1: Sketch Family Fun Into Your Weekly Plan (Yes, Literally)

Just like work, appointments, and chores… **fun needs a block.**

Otherwise, you'll hit Saturday night and realize everyone's been staring at their own screen for hours while you fold laundry and feel vaguely guilty.

Start with a **simple weekly sketch**:

- Friday night: Family movie
- Saturday afternoon: Outing or "yes" activity (everyone picks something)
- Sunday morning: Donuts after beach walk
- Weeknight "fun flash": 20-minute card game or silly video time

Even one or two intentional family blocks per week can **dramatically improve your family rhythm.**

It gives everyone something to look forward to.

It helps anchor your week with joy.

And it shifts the tone of your home from "what needs to get done" to "how can we connect today?"

In our house, we have "Fun Friday." That might mean frozen pizza and a show we all watch together, or driving through town to look at holiday lights, or playing a ridiculous game we make up. It's not complicated—but it's consistent. That's the secret.

2: Theme Your Fun (When You're Tired of Coming Up With Ideas)

Let's be honest—sometimes the hardest part of planning fun is the mental effort of figuring out what to do.

That's where **themed fun** comes in. You don't have to reinvent the wheel every time. Use go-to categories and plug them in based on your family's mood, weather, or energy level.

Try themes like:

- **Movie Night** (each person gets a pick every few weeks)
- **Game Night** (board games, card games, or made-up games—"What's In My Purse?" is a hit)
- **"Yes Night"** (within reason, everyone gets to choose something fun we do, eat, or play)
- **Try Something New Night** (a new recipe, activity, or place)
- **Outside Fun** (walk, hike, sidewalk chalk, backyard bonfire)

Sketch one per week. Keep a running list somewhere visible (fridge, whiteboard, your planner). When you hit decision fatigue, just point to the list and go, *"Let's do this one."*

3: Include the Family in the Planning

Here's the thing about planning family fun—you don't have to do it *for* your family. You can do it *with* them.

Let everyone have a say:

- Let your kids suggest activities for the weekend
- Have a "family fun jar" with ideas you pull out together
- Do a quick planning chat over Sunday dinner or Saturday breakfast
- Let each person "host" one night a month—they pick the movie, dinner, or game

You'll be surprised at how fun it becomes when everyone feels like part of the process (even if their idea of fun is 45 straight minutes of UNO chaos).

And as a bonus? You're teaching your kids **how to sketch time for joy**—a life skill they'll thank you for later.

4: Consider Energy + Season

Not every week is a *zoo trip and handmade pizza* kind of week. Some weeks, your version of family fun will be:

- Eating ice cream in pajamas on the couch
- Watching a 22-minute show together and calling it good
- Listening to a funny podcast while you all clean up the kitchen
- Drawing with sidewalk chalk while dinner's in the oven

The point is **not** to force fun into a tight box.

The point is to ask:

"What's something simple we can do together this week that fills us up?"

Use Sketch Planning to match the **activity to your energy.**

If it's a busy sports week? Keep it short and home-based.

If everyone's been extra stressed? Go for laughter, ease, or something outdoors.

If it's a holiday or birthday weekend? Maybe go bigger and plan a memory-maker.

Let the plan serve the season, not the other way around.

5: Reflect + Reset Weekly

After each week, take 60 seconds and ask:

- Did we have any meaningful family time?
- What worked? What felt forced or stressful?
- What would we want to do again next week?

Write it in your planner, talk about it at dinner, or just jot a note in your phone.

The goal isn't to build the perfect routine. It's to stay **mindful and connected**—and Sketch Planning helps you do exactly that.

Your Family Deserves Joy, Not Just Survival

There's always going to be laundry.

There's always going to be dishes.

There's always going to be one more email, one more appointment, one more thing to do.

But what your family will remember most?

- That one night you stayed up late watching a movie and laughing at the same part three times

- That moment in the car when everyone sang the chorus of an old Taylor Swift song at full volume
- That picnic on the living room floor
- That silly game that turned into a weekly ritual

Fun isn't extra. It's essential.

And now, you don't have to wait for it to magically happen.

You can **sketch it in, protect the space, and enjoy the people you love—on purpose.**

You've got the plan.

Now go make it joyful.

Handling Family Emergencies

Because no one plans for a trip to urgent care—but that doesn't mean your whole life has to unravel when it happens.

Let's get something straight: emergencies aren't just the big, dramatic, headline-worthy events.

Sometimes a "family emergency" looks like:

- Your toddler spiking a fever at 2 a.m.
- A frantic call from school about a forgotten inhaler

- A pipe bursting while you were on a Zoom call
- A missed alarm that derails your whole day
- A fight between siblings that leaves emotional wreckage and a broken LEGO set

It's not always life-threatening—but it's **life-disrupting**.

And when you're already stretched thin, even a small emergency can send you into survival mode.

That's why Sketch Planning isn't just about organizing the *ideal* week—it's about **building a flexible framework that supports you in the real, messy, chaotic moments too**.

Let's talk about how to navigate those unexpected events without falling apart.

First: Know That Flexibility Is Built In

Repeat this out loud (seriously):

"I am not failing because the plan changed."

If your default response to chaos is to blame yourself, I want you to stop. Right here. Right now.

Sketch Planning is intentionally **designed to flex**. It's not a strict to-do list. It's a roadmap that can reroute when necessary—without losing direction.

Think of it like this:

- When Google Maps hits traffic, it doesn't yell at you. It recalculates.
- That's exactly what your sketch is allowed to do.

The point isn't to stick to the plan. The point is to keep moving forward—even when life throws a detour at you.

1: Pause + Assess Without Panic

When something happens that throws your day (or week) into chaos, the first is to stop and breathe.

Ask yourself:

- What exactly changed?
- What time or energy will it affect today or this week?
- What needs to move?
- What can be dropped completely?
- What *still matters* today?

Instead of going into reactive mode—where you're putting out fires while spiraling about how much you're dropping—this simple pause helps you **respond instead of react.**

I've had days where the morning goes off the rails and the only thing that saved me from crying in the grocery store parking lot was asking, "Okay, what has to happen *now*, and what can wait until tomorrow?" It's not about being unshaken. It's about finding your footing when the ground shifts.

2: Resketch Your Day or Week

This is where the magic of Sketch Planning shines.

Because your plan isn't locked in stone—you can **resketch it** in five minutes.

Look at your Time Blocks and ask:

- Which blocks are totally off-limits now?
- Which blocks can be adjusted or shortened?
- Where is a Flex Block or overflow time I can use?

- Can I move a King to another day or replace it with an Easily Moved task?

Then redraw your sketch—mentally or literally—so you're no longer trying to follow a schedule that no longer fits.

This isn't falling behind.

This is **reorganizing with purpose.**

3: Communicate + Delegate Where You Can

When emergencies hit, we tend to default into *hyper-responsibility mode*—trying to keep everything going, solo, while handling the crisis.

But this is when support matters most.

So ask:

- Can your partner take over dinner tonight?
- Can a neighbor do the school run?
- Can the kids clean up their own mess while you handle the urgent stuff?
- Can you email your team/client/teacher to request grace or a deadline shift?

Asking for help is not weakness—it's wisdom.

Sketch Planning creates the clarity that lets you say:

"Hey, I need to move this. Here's why. Here's the new plan."

You're not flaking. You're being strategic.

4: Keep the Essentials—Drop the Extras

When you're in emergency mode, your only job is to **protect what matters most**.

Your Family Kings might shrink down to:

- Keep everyone fed
- Get through the next 24 hours
- Make sure the sick kid rests and the healthy ones feel secure
- Keep your sanity intact (even if that means screens, snacks, and cereal for dinner)

Anything else—laundry, inbox zero, vacuuming, that Pinterest-worthy holiday craft—can wait.

Give yourself permission to drop the "shoulds" and focus on **the musts**.

You'll pick the rest back up later, when life calms down. And it will.

5: Use a "Crisis Sketch" When Needed

Sometimes you're not dealing with a one-off emergency. Sometimes it's **a whole season**—a health scare, caregiving for a parent, a partner's job loss, or just a series of hard weeks that keep coming.

In those cases, create a simplified sketch. A "crisis mode" version of your routine.

That might mean:

- Two blocks per day instead of four
- Only sketching Family Kings and essential work tasks
- Using meal rotations or repeats (Taco Tuesday forever)
- Lowering expectations across the board for rest, flexibility, and grace

You're still Sketch Planning. You're just doing it with a gentler pencil.

6: Reflect After the Storm

Once the dust settles—whether it was a one-day derailment or a multi-week crisis—take a few minutes to reflect.

Ask:

- What helped me stay grounded?
- What didn't work, and why?
- What support or prep could help if this happens again?
- What can I do to restore calm this week?

This isn't about judgment—it's about gathering wisdom for the next time life throws a wrench (because let's be real... it will).

Maybe you create a list of emergency meals.

Maybe you prep a "family emergency block" each week just in case.

Maybe you realize you need more margin in your sketch during certain seasons.

Whatever it is—**you now have a tool to get back on track without shame.**

Calm Isn't the Absence of Chaos—It's the Ability to Move Through It

You can't stop life from being unpredictable.

But you *can* create a rhythm, a system, and a mindset that helps you stay calm, stay focused, and adapt with confidence—*not panic.*

Sketch Planning gives you that power.

It helps you:

- Pause
- Breathe
- Regroup

- Resketch
- Move forward

Not perfectly. But **peacefully**.

You don't need to do it all.

You just need to do what matters most right now—and trust that you'll pick up the rest when you're ready.

You're strong. You're capable. And you've got this.

(And if today all you did was keep everyone alive and semi-fed? That counts.)

Reviewing and Refining Family Plans

Because families grow, change, and go through weird phases—and your plan should too.

Family life is not static.

It shifts and stretches, often when you least expect it.

Your toddler who used to nap like a dream suddenly drops naps altogether.

Your tween starts joining every club, activity, and band practice in a 12-mile radius.

Your partner's work schedule changes. Your parents need more help. The dog starts barking every day at 3 p.m. for no reason.

The point is: **even the best family rhythm eventually needs a tune-up.**

That doesn't mean you failed—it means you're human. And your family is evolving, just like it's supposed to.

That's why **reviewing and refining your Sketch Plan is a built-in part of the system—not an afterthought.**

It helps you stay in sync, reduce stress, and keep the whole "life machine" humming with a little less clunk and a lot more calm.

First, Let Go of the Guilt Around "Changing the Plan"

There's a weird pressure that comes with "having a system"—like once we make a plan, we should stick to it *no matter what.*

But that's just not how real life works—especially in a house with multiple humans, unexpected events, growth spurts, emotions, and a snack schedule more demanding than a Michelin-star restaurant.

So let's reframe it:

Changing the plan isn't failure. It's family wisdom.

When you regularly review and refine your Sketch Plan, you're showing up *on purpose.*

You're listening. Adjusting. Growing together.

You're saying, *"I care enough about how we're living to make it better."*

That's not weakness. That's leadership.

1: Set a Weekly (or Bi-Weekly) Review Ritual

Just like you might review your budget or meal plan, set aside regular time to check in on your family rhythm.

This doesn't have to be formal. It can look like:

- A Sunday afternoon coffee and planner check-in

- A 10-minute convo during family dinner

- A solo "mom CEO moment" during your personal planning time

- A sticky note brainstorm session on the fridge

Ask yourself a few simple but powerful questions:

- What's working well in our current routine?
- What's consistently stressful or falling through the cracks?
- Are we getting enough family time together?
- Am I constantly overwhelmed by something that could be changed?

These questions help you catch what's *actually happening*—not what you *intended* to happen.

My Tip:

I do a quick review on Sunday night. I look at my Time Blocks from the past week, notice what kept getting bumped or forgotten, and ask, "Was this just a bad week, or is this a bad fit for our routine?" If it's the second one, I resketch. No shame.

2: Involve the Whole Family in the Process

You don't need to run a boardroom meeting with PowerPoint slides, but looping in your people—especially your kids—can create incredible awareness and harmony.

Try these:

- "What's something that's been hard or rushed this week?"
- "Is there something you'd like more time for?"
- "Is there a day that feels too full?"
- "What do you want to do as a family this week?"

Kids are surprisingly insightful when given the space to reflect. And even if they don't have big suggestions, *they'll feel heard.* That alone makes them more likely to engage with the routine you create together.

Pro Tip: Let kids sketch their own simple version of the plan—especially if they're neurodivergent or thrive with structure. It helps them take ownership and reduces the "Mom, what's next?" questions by about 67%.

3: Use Real-Life Feedback, Not Just Wishful Thinking

It's easy to plan a week based on **ideal energy and cooperation levels**.

In theory:

- You wake up early
- Everyone gets ready without drama
- Meals are smooth
- Kids go to bed on time
- You have space for family fun and alone time

In reality:

- Someone's sick
- Someone forgot their gym shoes (again)
- The dishwasher broke
- And bedtime turns into an emotional spiral

That's why it's so important to ask:

"How did this actually *feel* last week?"

Were mornings tense? Did the evening routine take forever? Did you forget the field trip permission slip because the sketch didn't include admin time?

Refining the plan means learning from your week—not punishing yourself for it.

4: Tweak One Area at a Time

It's tempting to overhaul the whole system when things feel chaotic. But major overhauls often don't stick—especially with kids and routines that are already ingrained.

Instead, choose **one focus area** per week or two:

- Tweak the morning routine
- Try a new way of handling chores
- Add a true "family fun" block
- Insert a recurring buffer before dinner
- Build in more space between activities

Small shifts lead to big results over time.

Sketch Planning gives you a visual map, so you can *see* if the new flow makes sense before you commit to it.

5: Protect the Wins

As you refine, don't forget to **celebrate what's working.**

Maybe you found the perfect time to do a weekly grocery run.

Maybe bedtime has become less of a battle.

Maybe your family walks after dinner are starting to become a favorite thing.

These are victories. Don't change them just because you're in "fix-it" mode.

Write them down. Highlight them. Protect them.

Because when life gets overwhelming again (and it will), you can come back to those little anchors and say, *"Okay, let's start here."*

Family Harmony Doesn't Come From Perfection—It Comes From Intention

There's no perfect schedule.

No one-size-fits-all planner.

No magic block that guarantees zero meltdowns or messes.

But there **is** a way to live with more clarity, connection, and calm.

And that comes from Sketch Planning:

- Pausing to see what's working
- Listening to your people
- Tweaking what's not
- And protecting what matters

When you review and refine regularly, you're not just managing time.

You're nurturing a home that feels good to live in—for everyone in it.

So don't be afraid to make changes.

Give yourself permission to adjust.

And trust that you're not behind—you're evolving. As you should be.

10

Advanced Sketch Planning Techniques: Mastering Efficiency

Timeboxing

Because "This will only take five minutes" is a lie we've all told ourselves.

You sit down to do one thing. Just one.

Answer a quick email. Fold a single basket of laundry. Tidy the kitchen counter.

Two hours later, you've deep-cleaned the fridge, reorganized three drawers, and you forgot what the original task even was.

Sound familiar?

Yeah... you're not alone.

Because tasks have a sneaky way of *expanding* to fill whatever time you give them. It's called **Parkinson's Law**—and it's very real. Left unsupervised, even the smallest chore can become a time-consuming monster that hijacks your whole day.

That's where **Timeboxing** comes in.

Timeboxing is the practice of assigning a specific start and end time to a task—and *sticking to it.* It's like giving your to-dos a playpen. They're allowed to exist... but only within boundaries.

Let's break down how to use Timeboxing as part of your Sketch Planning routine so your days feel productive, not stolen by socks, scrolls, or unexpected side quests.

First: Why Timeboxing Works (Even If You're Not a "Strict Schedule" Person)

Timeboxing is not about creating a rigid, minute-by-minute schedule.

It's about **setting healthy boundaries with your time**—so you stay focused, finish things faster, and avoid spending your entire afternoon cleaning the baseboards because you fell into a distraction spiral.

Here's what Timeboxing helps you do:

- Stay on task (you know when to stop)
- Avoid perfectionism (you can't endlessly "tweak")
- Feel accomplished (because something *got done*, not just started)
- Protect your energy (so one task doesn't eat your whole day)
- Create *realistic* plans that actually fit in your Sketch

It gives you permission to stop... even if the task isn't "perfect."

(Yes, even if the towels don't match. It's okay. Let it go, Elsa.)

1: Choose Tasks That Need Boundaries

Not every task needs a box. But many benefit from it—especially the ones that tend to:

- Take longer than expected
- Spiral into extra work
- Feel never-ending or open-ended
- Drain your energy when left undefined

These often include:

- Email or admin tasks
- House cleaning
- Errands
- Social media or content creation
- Meal prep
- Project work
- Brainstorming sessions
- Creative work (because the ideas never "end," right?)

Pick 1–3 tasks per day to Timebox. Not everything—just the ones that need a leash.

2: Assign Time Limits in Your Sketch Plan

Timeboxing works beautifully inside your existing Time Blocks.

Instead of filling a whole 3-hour block with vague to-dos, you assign **specific time limits** to each key task.

Example: Afternoon Block (1–4 PM)

- 1:00–1:30 PM: Respond to emails (Timeboxed)
- 1:30–2:15 PM: Fold & put away laundry (Timeboxed)
- 2:15–3:00 PM: Sketch content plan (Timeboxed)
- 3:00–3:45 PM: School pickup + decompress

Notice: there's space to breathe, and each task knows **when it ends.**

That means if it's 1:30 and you're still knee-deep in your inbox, the buzzer goes off and you *move on*.

(Yes, even if you didn't answer the sixth email about the school bake sale. It'll be fine.)

3: Use Timers, Alarms, or Visual Cues

Timeboxing works best when you actually... you know, **keep track of time.**

Try one of these:

- Set a timer on your phone
- Use a visual countdown clock (great if you're a visual learner or neuro-divergent)
- Try the Pomodoro Technique (25 min work, 5 min break)
- Use a playlist as a timer—"I'll stop when this album ends"
- Put your planner or task list somewhere visible as an anchor

This isn't about pressure—it's about focus.

Bonus Tip: If you're easily distracted, sketch a 5-minute "buffer" before or after your timeboxed task to handle detours, interruptions, or snack breaks. Because life.

4: When the Timer Goes Off, Stop (Seriously, Stop)

This is the hardest part.

Because sometimes the task isn't "done."

Sometimes you feel like if you just had 10 more minutes...

But the whole point of Timeboxing is to train your brain to **respect your time.**

To say, *"This is how much I'm giving this task. That's enough for now."*

If it's not finished, you can:

- Schedule a follow-up block later in the week
- Add it to a Flex Block
- Or—radical thought—*decide that it's good enough for now*

Even unfinished tasks can be "complete" for today.

The more you practice stopping on time, the more control you build over your day.

And trust me: that feels *amazing.*

5: Reflect + Adjust for Future Sketches

At the end of your day or week, ask:

- Did my time limits feel realistic?
- Did I under- or over-estimate certain tasks?
- What threw me off—and how can I prep for that next time?
- What felt *really* good and focused?

You'll learn so much about your personal work pace, energy cycles, and where time tends to leak out.

This is how your Sketch Plan gets smarter.

More accurate. More doable. More *you.*

If I don't timebox certain tasks, I will absolutely spend way too long "tweaking" graphics, scrolling Pinterest for recipe inspiration, or trying to declutter one drawer only to find myself reorganizing the entire bathroom by accident.

So I've learned to sketch things like:

- "Clean bathroom – 25 min max"
- "Plan next week's blog – 45 min cap"
- "Social content – 30 min and DONE (no rabbit holes allowed)"

And when that timer goes off, I get up, grab coffee, and move on—even if it's not "perfect."

Because done-ish is still better than burnt out.

You Can Do More—By Doing Less, On Purpose

Timeboxing isn't about squeezing more into your day.

It's about *freeing your brain from time anxiety.*

You're not winging it.

You're not getting lost in the weeds.

You're being intentional.

And when your time has boundaries?

So does your stress.

You're not meant to push all day.

You're meant to show up, give it your best, and then—*let it be enough.*

With Sketch Planning and Timeboxing working together, your tasks stay in their lane... and your peace of mind stays intact.

The Pomodoro Technique

Because you can do anything for 25 minutes—even that thing you've been avoiding for two weeks.

Let's be real: it's hard to focus for long periods of time when you've got kids, pets, work, laundry buzzing, school emails coming in, and a brain that won't stop spinning.

Some days, you barely have time to finish your coffee before someone needs a snack, a sock, or help opening a juice pouch that was clearly designed by an evil engineer.

And yet... there's still stuff that needs doing.

Whether it's writing, cleaning, planning, or emailing—you've got tasks that require actual brainpower. And focus.

That's where the **Pomodoro Technique** comes in.

This method is beautifully simple, surprisingly effective, and *100% Sketch Planning approved.*

Let's dig into how it works—and why it might be the secret weapon your schedule's been missing.

What Is the Pomodoro Technique?

No, it's not a pasta recipe (although pasta is always a good idea).

The Pomodoro Technique is a time management method developed by Francesco Cirillo in the 1980s. He named it after the tomato-shaped kitchen timer he used while studying (pomodoro is Italian for "tomato").

Here's the basic idea:

1. Pick one task.
2. Set a timer for **25 minutes**.
3. Work on that task—and *only* that task—until the timer goes off.
4. Take a **5-minute break**.
5. Repeat the cycle. After 4 Pomodoros, take a longer break (15–30 minutes).

That's it. It's beautifully low-tech, low-pressure, and totally doable—even on your busiest days.

Why It Works (Especially for Overwhelmed Brains)

There are a few reasons this method is wildly effective:

- **It lowers the starting barrier.**
- Instead of thinking "I have to work for 2 hours," your brain hears "Just 25 minutes." That feels doable—even if the task feels huge.
- **It trains your brain to focus in short, sustainable bursts.**
- You're not fighting to stay on task for hours—you're giving your brain permission to sprint, then rest.
- **It helps reduce perfectionism.**

- You don't have to *finish* the whole thing. You just have to work on it for 25 minutes. That's enough for now.
- **It creates a natural rhythm.**
- Work, rest, repeat. You're not burning out—you're pacing yourself.
- **It works with real-life interruptions.**
- If your kid needs something after 18 minutes? Fine. Pause. Restart later. It's a flexible system, not a rigid rulebook.

How to Use the Pomodoro Technique in Sketch Planning

Pomodoros fit beautifully into your Time Blocks—especially when a task needs your full attention.

Let's say you sketch a 2-hour Work Block in the afternoon.

Instead of writing:

"Write blog post 2:00–4:00"

Try: **Work Block (2:00–4:00)**

- 2:00–2:25 – Pomodoro 1: Draft outline
- 2:25–2:30 – Break
- 2:30–2:55 – Pomodoro 2: Write intro and section one
- 2:55–3:00 – Break
- 3:00–3:25 – Pomodoro 3: Write remaining sections
- 3:25–3:30 – Break
- 3:30–4:00 – Flex/review/edit or wrap up

Instead of drifting or doom-scrolling halfway through, you're moving with purpose. And breaks are *built in*—no guilt attached.

I use Pomodoros when I'm staring down something I really don't want to do—like updating a course module, writing email copy I've put off, or doing a cleaning task I've been avoiding for, oh, three weeks.

I tell myself:

"Just one Pomodoro. Just 25 minutes. I don't have to finish—I just have to start."

Nine times out of ten?

I find my flow. I feel better. And even if I don't finish the whole thing, I've made real progress.

Sometimes that first Pomodoro is all I need. Other times I stack two or three together—and suddenly I've done more in 75 minutes than I would've done with 3 hours of "sort of working while checking my phone."

How to Make It Work for You

You don't need anything fancy to do Pomodoros, but a little setup helps.

Here's what I recommend:

- Use a simple timer (kitchen, phone, or app like Focus Keeper or Be Focused)
- Put your phone on Do Not Disturb or in another room
- Keep a notepad nearby to jot down unrelated thoughts ("Oh yeah, I need to order dog food") so they don't distract you
- Set the vibe—music, silence, whatever helps you focus
- Tell your kids/partner, "I'm doing a 25-minute focus sprint. Unless it's

urgent, wait until I'm done." (It doesn't always work, but hey—it helps.)

Then dive in.

Give it your full focus.

And when the timer goes off—*stop* and rest.

Even if it's just a walk to the kitchen for water or a scroll break (if that energizes you). Your brain needs that breath.

Pomodoro Modifications for Real Life

We're moms. We don't always get a full 25 minutes uninterrupted, and that's okay.

Try these variations:

- **The Baby Pomodoro:** 10–15 minutes if your brain or schedule is fried
- **The "Stacked Sprint":** Two 25-minute rounds back to back when you're on a roll
- **Kid-Friendly Pomodoros:** Set a timer and challenge your child to do homework, clean, or read for the same time you're working—they love the race!
- **Chore Pomodoros:** "I'll clean the kitchen for 25 minutes and *then I'm done today.*" That boundary changes everything.

The point is: *work with your life, not against it.*

Small Bursts Make a Big Difference

You don't need giant blocks of time.

You don't need perfect focus.

You don't need to finish everything in one sitting.

You just need **25 minutes of intention.**

That's it.

The Pomodoro Technique isn't about hustle—it's about *honoring your time and energy* in a way that actually works for your real life.

One task. One timer. One tiny commitment.

And that? That's enough to keep moving forward—even when life is loud, messy, and full of socks that somehow never end up in pairs.

You're doing great. Keep going.

Batching Similar Tasks

Because switching from writing an email to unloading the dishwasher to texting the babysitter is basically a workout for your frontal lobe—and it's exhausting.

Let's talk about **mental residue**.

Every time you switch tasks—especially between different types of tasks—you lose a little bit of energy.

It's why jumping from writing to dishes to a meeting to Instagram to homework help makes your brain feel like *mashed potatoes by 2 p.m.*

That mental drag? It adds up fast.

Enter: **Task Batching**.

One of the easiest, most powerful ways to simplify your day, reduce overwhelm, and actually *get stuff done faster.*

Think of batching as your brain's favorite life hack—it's like cleaning all the bathrooms at once instead of one a day, or replying to all your texts in one go instead of awkwardly spacing them out over five hours (guilty).

Let's break down how to use batching inside your Sketch Planning system to make your days feel smoother, lighter, and way more productive.

What Is Task Batching?

Batching means **grouping similar tasks together** and doing them in one focused block of time.

So instead of:

- Responding to an email at 9:07
- Cleaning out your inbox again at 10:45
- And replying to one more message at 3:15...

You batch it:

"Answer emails from 11:00–11:30."

Same with chores.

Instead of doing one load of laundry Monday, vacuuming Tuesday, dusting Wednesday—you batch:

"Clean house Tuesday morning for 90 minutes."

You're not doing *more*. You're doing the same amount of work—just smarter.

Because you're reducing the mental cost of switching gears over and over and over again.

Why Batching Works (Especially for Busy Moms)

- **Less decision fatigue**
- You're not constantly asking, "What should I do next?" You've already grouped it.
- **More flow**

- When you're doing one type of task (all writing, all errands, all cleaning), you get into a rhythm. That's where the magic happens.
- **Fewer open loops**
- You close one whole category at a time, instead of leaving little half-finished things all over your brain.
- **Reduced distractions**
- When you know you'll *get to it later*, it's easier to stay focused now.
- **Mental peace**
- Your brain finally gets a break from trying to hold everything at once.

How to Batch Inside Your Sketch Plan

Let's say you have a 3-hour block open in the afternoon.

Instead of plugging in ten different tasks, pick one category—and do everything related to that theme.

Example: Tuesday Afternoon (1:00–4:00 PM)

Admin Batch

- Answer emails
- Respond to DMs
- Check school calendar
- Pay bills
- Order birthday gift

- Refill dog food order
- Confirm dentist appointment

All admin. All handled. No task-switching required.

Other batching categories might include:

- **Content Batch:** Write blog post, plan Instagram captions, schedule newsletter
- **Housework Batch:** Laundry, clean bathroom, dust, vacuum
- **Errand Batch:** Grocery run, post office, Target pickup
- **Meal Batch:** Chop veggies, prep lunches, freeze dinner, clean out fridge
- **Planning Batch:** Sketch next week, meal plan, check calendar, prep to-do list
- **Creative Batch:** Brainstorm course ideas, design freebies, write workbook pages
- **Family Batch:** Family fun night, chore board update, kids' paperwork, one-on-one time

Batching has been a game-changer for me—especially with things like email and housework. If I don't batch email, I'm checking it all day, reacting constantly, and never actually finishing anything.

Now I sketch email batching blocks 3 times a week—and outside those blocks? I let it sit. That boundary is GOLD.

Same with cleaning. I used to "just tidy up real quick" multiple times a day. Now I batch the major cleaning on set days, and it feels so much lighter. No more endless micro-tasks lurking in the background.

How to Start Batching (Without Overhauling Everything)

Start small.

You don't need to batch every single area of your life starting tomorrow. (Please don't.)

Pick one area where task-switching is stealing your energy. Try a batching block there and see how it feels.

Start here:

- What types of tasks do you repeat throughout the week?
- Which ones could be grouped together?
- What day or time feels best to batch them?

Then sketch it into your plan:

- "Admin Hour – Wednesday 10:00 AM"
- "House Batch – Saturday morning"
- "Content Batch – Monday 1:00–3:00 PM"

That's it. That's the move.

What to Avoid When Batching

- **Overpacking your batch.**
- Keep your batching list realistic—5–6 tasks max. Otherwise, it turns into a mental avalanche.

- **Forgetting breaks.**
- Just because the tasks are similar doesn't mean you won't need a breather. Add a 5–10 minute buffer if your batch is longer than 60–90 minutes.
- **Trying to multitask.**
- Batching only works when you *focus on one category.* Don't sneak in a chore mid-email batch. (I see you.)

Bonus: Weekly Batching Anchors

Once you find your rhythm, try building **weekly batching themes** into your Sketch Plan.

Example:

- **Monday:** Planning + Creative
- **Tuesday:** Housework
- **Wednesday:** Admin + Appointments
- **Thursday:** Work Projects or Client Tasks
- **Friday:** Light Flex or Errands
- **Saturday:** Family + Fun
- **Sunday:** Reset + Prep

It's not about following this perfectly—it's about giving your week structure that *supports* you, not exhausts you.

You're Not Behind—You're Just Too Scattered

You don't need to hustle harder.

You don't need more motivation.

You don't need a color-coded 12-checklist.

You just need a better flow.

Batching brings that flow back.

It simplifies your plan. Calms your brain. Saves your energy. And lets you finish things faster—without the constant "what was I doing again?" fog.

So go ahead—group it, sketch it, knock it out in one clean swipe.

Your brain (and your to-do list) will thank you.

The Two-Minute Rule

Because if it takes less time to do it than to stress about it—you might as well just do it.

Here's a scenario we all know too well:

You walk by a basket of unfolded laundry.

You think, *"I'll get to that later."*

Later turns into tomorrow.

Then someone needs socks.

Now you're digging through the basket in mild panic while mumbling to yourself and questioning your life choices.

That's the power of small tasks: they're deceptively simple... but when left undone, they snowball into stress, guilt, and mess.

The good news? There's an incredibly easy way to stop that from happening.

It's called **The Two-Minute Rule**, and it might just change the way you manage your time (and your brain).

What Is the Two-Minute Rule?

The Two-Minute Rule is simple:

If a task takes two minutes or less to do—do it right now.

That's it.

No overthinking. No adding it to a list. No mental back-and-forth.

Just... *do the thing.*

This concept comes from productivity expert David Allen, creator of the *Getting Things Done* method. And while the original version focuses on inboxes and work, it translates beautifully to real life—especially busy mom life.

Because when you're juggling work, kids, home, errands, relationships, and your own basic hygiene... those "quick little things" can add up fast. And become *mental clutter* even faster.

Why It Works (And Why It's So Dang Satisfying)

Here's what makes the Two-Minute Rule powerful:

- **It prevents pile-ups.**

- Two-minute tasks are like tiny messes—easy to clean up now, annoying to face later.

- **It clears mental space.**

- Crossing things off your list quickly feels *amazing.* One less thing bouncing around in your head.

- **It creates momentum.**

- Doing one thing leads to another. It's the productivity snowball—without the avalanche.

- **It reduces resistance.**
- There's no room for "should I or shouldn't I?" You just act. Which is *way less exhausting* than indecision.

What Kinds of Tasks Qualify?

Anything that takes **two minutes or less** to complete. Here are some examples:

- Putting shoes away instead of walking past them
- Texting someone back
- Responding to a quick email
- Tossing a wrapper instead of setting it down
- Wiping the counter
- Replacing the toilet paper roll
- Refilling the dog's water bowl
- Throwing something in the laundry instead of piling it "for later"
- Adding an event to the calendar *now* instead of relying on memory

These are the things that don't *seem* urgent... until they stack up into a big ol' pile of stress.

The Two-Minute Rule has saved my mornings more times than I can count.

Instead of letting the small things wait and build up, I've trained myself to just *do them while I'm already moving.*

If I pass the dishwasher and it's done? I open it. I don't overthink it—I just unload a few things right then. If the library book is sitting by the door? I toss it in the car now, not later. And if I remember something during dinner cleanup? I voice note myself or scribble it down in my sketch before I forget.

It's not about perfection. It's about *lightening the load* in little ways that *add up big time.*

How to Build It Into Your Sketch Plan

The Two-Minute Rule doesn't need its own block—it fits *inside* your day.

Use it like this:

- During a Time Block: Start with a couple 2-minute tasks to warm up.
- As a transition tool: Knock out a few small wins between bigger tasks.
- As part of your evening reset: Spend 5 minutes doing 2-minute tasks to start the next day cleaner.
- In your Admin Blocks: Clear 2-minute to-dos before diving into deeper work.

Example: Before your Work Block begins

- Put away laundry on the bed
- Set out dinner ingredients
- Text your sister back
- Refill your water bottle

- = Four quick wins, zero buildup.

What to Watch Out For (Yes, Even This Has Boundaries)

As powerful as this rule is, it has a couple caveats:

- **Don't let it derail deep work.**
- If you're in a Pomodoro or Timebox, jot the 2-minute task down and return later. *Not everything needs to be done instantly.*
- **Don't expand it.**
- Keep it tight. Folding *one shirt* = yes. Deciding to re-sort the whole closet = no. Don't let a tiny task become a productivity rabbit hole.
- **Don't guilt yourself.**
- This rule is a tool, not a weapon. It's okay to say "I'll do that in my reset block" if you're too drained right now.

Bonus Tip: Stack Your 2-Minuters

If you're feeling scattered but not ready for a big task, sketch a **Two-Minute Power Burst.**

Example:

"10-Minute Power Sweep: Do 5 two-minute tasks in a row. Let's go."

Set a timer and knock out:

- Recycle junk mail
- Start the washing machine
- Take vitamins

- Wipe the bathroom mirror
- Fill out the permission slip

Boom. Five things off your plate in under 10 minutes. You're a rockstar.

Small Tasks Matter, Too

Sometimes we wait to feel "productive" until we've done something big.

But real life? Real life is *made* of small moments and quick wins.

The Two-Minute Rule is a gentle reminder that:

- You don't have to do everything.
- You don't have to do it later.
- You *can* feel accomplished with just a few quick moves.

Because progress isn't always giant.

Sometimes, it's just putting the dish in the sink *right now.*

And that? That counts.

Eisenhower Matrix

Because everything feels urgent when you're the default parent—but not everything deserves your energy.

If you've ever felt like you worked all day but have *no clue what you actually accomplished...*

Or like your to-do list has turned into a hydra that grows two new tasks every time you check one off...

You're not alone.

The problem isn't that you're not working hard enough.

It's that most of us are spending our energy in the **wrong quadrants**.

And the reason?

We haven't been taught how to **prioritize based on value**, not just volume.

That's what makes the Eisenhower Matrix so powerful—it gives you a simple, visual way to take control of your time and attention so you can work smarter, not just harder.

A Quick Refresher: What Is the Eisenhower Matrix?

Named after President Dwight D. Eisenhower, this matrix divides tasks into four categories based on two questions:

1. Is this task **urgent** (time-sensitive, needs immediate attention)?
2. Is this task **important** (connected to your long-term goals, values, or priorities)?

Here's what that looks like:

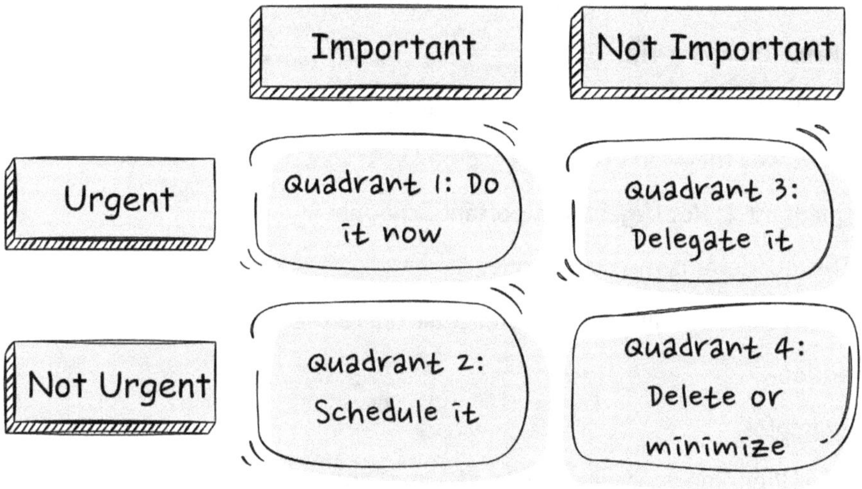

Each quadrant tells you *not just what to do*, but *how to approach it.*

Let's break them down with real-mom examples (because this is where the clarity really clicks).

Quadrant 1: Urgent + Important Do It Now

This is your **"fires to put out" zone.**

These tasks are both **time-sensitive and critical**, and ignoring them has real consequences.

Think:

- Your child gets hurt and needs care now
- You missed a deadline and need to fix it before it escalates
- You're about to run out of a critical medication
- The fridge broke and your groceries are melting

In this quadrant, it's all about **triage and action**. You deal with these tasks immediately—but you don't want to live here 24/7.

Too much time in Q1 = chronic stress, reactive mode, burnout.

Sketch Planning Tip:

Build margin into your week (Flex Blocks!) to handle these when they pop up. That way they don't completely derail your day.

Quadrant 2: Not Urgent + Important Schedule It

This quadrant is the **magic zone.**

It's full of the things that build a better future but rarely shout for your attention.

Examples:

- Planning your week (hello, Sketch Plan!)
- Spending quality time with your family
- Getting enough sleep
- Working on a personal or business goal
- Doing therapy, journaling, reading, resting
- Prepping meals so your week flows easier
- Creating a new routine that actually supports your mental health

This is where life-changing progress happens.

But because it's not urgent, it gets ignored... until something breaks (hello, Q1 again).

Sketch Planning Tip:

Your Time Blocks should be packed with Q2 activities. These are your Kings. Make space for them before anything else.

Quadrant 3: Urgent + Not Important Delegate It

This quadrant feels urgent—but it's **not aligned with your goals or well-being.** It's urgent to *someone else*, or maybe just *feels* urgent because of external pressure.

Examples:

- Replying to a "can you do this real quick?" text
- Being guilted into volunteering (again)
- Social media notifications or "urgent" but low-value work tasks
- Running an errand someone else could handle
- Answering every email the second it arrives

These tasks aren't evil—but they're sneaky. They give you the illusion of being busy and productive, when really they're keeping you from your actual priorities.

Sketch Planning Tip:

Learn to say "no" or "not now." Delegate what you can. Set boundaries—lovingly, clearly, and unapologetically.

My personal example:

I used to say yes to every little thing—school signups, friend favors, last-minute "can you just..." requests. I felt helpful, but I was running myself into the ground. Now I pause and ask, *"Is this my priority or someone else's fire?"* If it's Q3, I delegate or decline.

Quadrant 4: Not Urgent + Not Important Delete It

This is the **"waste zone."**

The tasks here aren't urgent, and they don't really matter—yet we do them all the time, especially when we're tired, avoiding something, or stuck in perfectionist mode.

Examples:

- Reorganizing your apps for the third time
- Scrolling Instagram for 30 minutes (then forgetting why you opened it)
- Rewriting your grocery list with better handwriting
- Reading every review before buying a $12 item
- Worrying about things you can't control

Now don't get me wrong—**true rest belongs in Q2, not Q4.**

The difference? Q2 rest is intentional. Q4 activity is usually just avoidance dressed up as productivity.

Sketch Planning Tip:

When you notice you're zoning out, gently ask yourself: *"Am I avoiding something that matters more?"* Then go resketch your plan to include a real break—and come back to the task refreshed.

How to Use the Matrix with Your Sketch Plan

1. **Do a Brain Dump**
2. Take 5 minutes to write down everything on your mind. Don't filter.
3. **Sort Into Quadrants**
4. Draw the matrix or label each task Q1–Q4. Use colored pens if that brings you joy. (We love that.)
5. **Sketch Accordingly**

- Q1 Today's Time Blocks

- Q2 Scheduled blocks throughout the week
- Q3 Delegate, batch, or drop
- Q4 Let it go, Elsa

Bonus: Add little symbols or stickers in your planner to track which quadrant tasks belong to. You'll start to notice patterns—and shift your focus naturally over time.

Real Talk: Why This Matters So Much for Moms

As moms, we're often living in Q1 and Q3:

- Putting out fires
- Managing others' priorities
- Responding to the loudest need in the moment

Which means Q2 (the soul-nourishing, peace-building quadrant) gets... forgotten.

The Eisenhower Matrix is your permission slip to:

- Stop treating everything like an emergency
- Say no without guilt
- Choose purpose over pressure
- And finally do the things that matter most to *you*

You're Not Behind—You Just Need a Better Filter

You are doing so much.

But not everything deserves your energy.

With the Eisenhower Matrix, you can finally look at your week and say:

"This matters now. This can wait. That? That's not mine to carry."

And suddenly?

You're not drowning in to-dos.

You're *leading your life with clarity.*

You've got this. And your Sketch Plan is going to reflect that.

11

Overcoming Procrastination: Strategies for Action

Understanding Procrastination

Because "I'll do it later" doesn't make you lazy—it means something's getting in your way.

Let's start with this truth bomb:

Procrastination is not a character flaw.

It's not proof that you're "not motivated" or "can't get it together."

It's not something you should be ashamed of.

And it's definitely not fixed by a fancy planner or yelling at yourself to "just focus already."

Procrastination is usually a sign that something deeper is going on:

- A fear

- A block
- An emotional wall
- Or maybe just *life exhaustion*

The task may look simple on the outside... but to your nervous system? It feels like a minefield. So your brain does what it's wired to do—it protects you by avoiding the thing that feels hard.

And then you feel frustrated, disappointed, guilty... and stuck.

Which leads to more avoiding.

And the cycle repeats.

Let's break that cycle—not with pressure, but with understanding.

First: What Is Procrastination Really?

Procrastination is the **act of delaying something** even though you know it needs to be done and you'll probably feel worse the longer you put it off.

Here's what it's *not*:

- Laziness
- Indecision
- A moral failure
- You being "bad" at life

Here's what it *is*:

- An emotional avoidance tactic
- A response to fear, anxiety, perfectionism, or overwhelm
- A protection mechanism that worked once—and now shows up by

default

Think of it like your brain's misguided attempt to keep you safe.

You *don't* want to deal with the uncomfortable feelings that might come up when doing the task... so your brain says, "Let's just scroll Pinterest for 'dinner ideas' instead." (Even though no one in your house eats quinoa.)

Sound familiar?

Real-Life Mom Moment: The Laundry Example

Let's say your laundry is piling up.

You walk past the same overflowing basket 4 times a day, each time thinking, *"Ugh, I really should deal with that."*

But instead, you check your email.

Then get distracted by a snack request.

Then a text. Then your brain tells you it's not the right time.

Then... it's 10 p.m. and you've still got Mount Washmore staring you down.

You didn't avoid it because you're lazy.

You avoided it because it felt like **too much**—mentally, physically, emotionally.

Maybe you were tired. Maybe you didn't want to start something you knew you couldn't finish. Maybe you were afraid that folding laundry meant facing a bigger list of all the other things you were behind on.

It's *never just the task.*

It's what the task represents.

Identifying the Triggers: Why You Might Be Procrastinating

Here's a deeper look at the *real reasons* we delay tasks—and what they often sound like inside our heads.

1. Overwhelm

You look at the task and feel instant mental fog. There's just *so much*—you freeze.

Inner dialogue:

"I don't even know where to start."

"This will take forever."

"If I start, I'll have to finish—and I can't right now."

Try this:

- Do a brain dump of the task. Break it into micro-steps.
- Sketch the first *tiny* step—just five minutes. You don't have to finish. You just have to *start*.

2. Perfectionism

You're not avoiding the task—you're avoiding doing it *imperfectly*.

Inner dialogue:

"What if it's not good enough?"

"If I can't do it right, I shouldn't do it at all."

"It needs to be perfect. I'll wait until I have more time."

Try this:

- Set a "done is better than perfect" timer (Pomodoro style)
- Remind yourself: 80% finished is still 100% more progress than 0%

My real talk:

I've rewritten the same email three times before because it "didn't sound quite right." I now give myself a 25-minute Timebox and say, "Get the first draft out. You can tweak it later—but it has to exist first."

3. Lack of Clarity

You're not sure what to do—or how to do it. So you stall.

Inner dialogue:

"I don't even know where to begin."

"What does 'launch the thing' even mean?"

"I'll just wait until I have a better plan."

Try this:

- Turn vague tasks into specific ones (e.g. "Write blog post" "Outline 3 points")
- Use batching to group "unclear" items and tackle them with fresh energy

4. Fear of Failure (or Success)

What if you mess up? What if it works and people expect more from you?

Inner dialogue:

"If I try and fail, I'll feel worse than if I never tried."

"Success means more pressure next time. I'm not ready for that."

Try this:

- Reframe success as experimentation. You're *testing*, not proving.
- Remind yourself: You're allowed to grow slowly. You don't need to nail it on round one.

5. Boredom / Task Aversion

It's just not interesting. It's repetitive. It's draining.

Inner dialogue:

"Ugh, not this again."

"I'd rather do literally anything else."

"Why am I always the one doing this?"

Try this:

- Set a timer (Pomodoro or 10-min block)
- Add music, a podcast, or a "reward" to go with the task
- Sketch it into your lowest-focus energy block—don't waste high brain-power here

6. Low Energy or Burnout

You're not procrastinating. You're **exhausted**.

Inner dialogue:

"I just can't think right now."

"I'm too tired to focus."

"If one more thing gets added, I'm going to cry."

Try this:

- Move the task to a high-energy window later
- Insert a Break Block or Flex Block
- Be honest: *Do I need rest more than I need to finish this?* If so, prioritize rest.

Breaking the Cycle: What to Do When You're Stuck

When you catch yourself procrastinating, try this 5-minute reframe:

1. **Pause and breathe**
2. Say it with me: "I am not lazy. I am not behind. I am just stuck." That's okay.

3. **Ask what you're avoiding**

4. Is it discomfort? Confusion? Pressure? Figure out the *real* reason.

5. **Shrink the task**

6. What's the tiniest you could take in 5 minutes? Do *just that.*

7. **Sketch the next step**

8. Give the task a time + place in your Sketch Plan. Not "later." Not "someday." *This week.*

9. **Celebrate starting**

10. Even if you didn't finish—starting is success. Momentum is magic.

Grace First, Then Structure

You don't overcome procrastination by "trying harder."

You overcome it by **understanding yourself better**.

Sketch Planning helps by giving you a visual structure—but more importantly, it helps you sketch with self-awareness.

You're not failing. You're not falling behind.

You just need a system that includes your real-life emotions and limitations—and honors your energy, not fights it.

So go ahead. Shrink the task. Sketch the plan. Start small.

And remember: *your worth is not defined by your productivity.*

You've got this.

Breaking Down Large Tasks

Because Rome wasn't built in a day—and neither is your launch, your house, or your meal plan.

Let's face it: big tasks are intimidating.

Even when you want to do them—even when they're exciting, or important, or things you've been dreaming about—they still have a way of making your brain freeze up like a toddler mid-tantrum. Arms crossed. Eyebrows raised. Full-body *nope* energy.

Because your brain isn't just seeing a task—it's seeing **an entire mountain** of to-dos, unknowns, time demands, and emotional load. And that mountain? It feels like too much.

So, what happens?

You avoid it. You push it to "later." You write it on the list five days in a row without touching it. You clean your pantry instead. You *research* the thing, but don't do the thing. You say things like "I just need a big chunk of time to focus," and then secretly hope that chunk of time never shows up so you don't have to face the mountain.

Sound familiar? Me too.

That's why breaking big tasks down into *tiny, doable pieces* is a core pillar of Sketch Planning. Because we're not here for the hustle. We're here to get stuff done in a way that fits into real life—with kids, dogs, dishes, and days that never go as planned.

The Mental Weight of "Big Tasks"

Big tasks aren't just time-consuming—they're emotionally heavy.

Think about it:

- **"Create a course"** could mean planning, filming, editing, designing, uploading, selling... yikes.
- **"Launch a new product"** sounds exciting... until your brain starts worrying about branding, copy, tech, timelines, and rejection.
- **"Plan Christmas"** seems joyful—until you remember the 49 sub-steps it actually involves: gifts, cards, travel, meals, Elf on the Shelf, keeping the kids alive while doing all of the above...

When you write that one massive task down on your planner, you're not creating clarity—you're creating *pressure*.

And that pressure? It turns into procrastination. Not because you don't care, but because your brain doesn't know where to start.

So let's give it a place to start.

1: Name the Big Task—and Define What It *Really* Means

Start by asking:

"What does this actually include?"

Let's say the task is:

"Start a blog."

Your brain sees that and panics because it's *not one task*—it's about 17.

Break it down:

1. Pick a name
2. Buy the domain
3. Set up hosting

4. Install WordPress or another platform

5. Choose a theme

6. Write your first post

7. Set up an email opt-in

8. Share on Pinterest

Now you've turned one massive, overwhelming blob into a series of manageable steps. Suddenly, you can sketch *"buy domain"* into tomorrow's Admin Block, and you've got momentum.

And that's the secret: **momentum > motivation.**

2: Chunk It Into Categories

If a task has a lot of moving parts, group them by theme.

For example, if you're prepping a launch:

- **Creative:** Write the sales page, record videos

- **Admin:** Set up cart, test checkout, schedule emails

- **Promotion:** Create graphics, write social captions, plan affiliate emails

Each category gets its own Focus Block on different days—no trying to do everything at once. No "this will only take 10 minutes" lies. Just clean containers for clear thinking.

When I break down big projects this way, I can sketch the "heavy brain" tasks into my mid-morning blocks (when I'm at my best), and save the admin stuff for late afternoon when my brain is toast. That way, I'm not fighting against my own energy cycles.

3: Estimate the Time for Each Piece

This is important.

Most of us either:

- Overestimate ("This will take hours!" when it could take 20 minutes), or
- Underestimate ("I'll just knock this out real quick," then it's 2 hours and 3 cups of coffee later)

So be realistic. Ask:

- How long does this *actually* take?
- Do I need full focus or can I multitask it?
- Is this a Timebox candidate? A Pomodoro sprint? A Flex task?

Then *sketch it accordingly.*

Pro Tip: If it's under 10 minutes, consider doing it immediately (Two-Minute Rule). If it's 20–45 minutes, Timebox it. If it needs full creativity, pair it with your highest-energy time of day.

4: Shrink the First Until It's Ridiculously Easy

If you're still stuck, the first is too big. Shrink it again.

Instead of:

"Record lesson one"

Try:

"Write 3 bullet points for lesson one outline"

Instead of:

"Clean the garage"

Try:

"Put empty boxes in recycling bin"

Instead of:

"Plan party"

Try:

"Text 3 friends to ask about availability"

Tiny steps create **psychological wins**. Your brain feels successful, which creates dopamine, which builds motivation. And guess what? That's what keeps you going.

5: Sketch It In—Don't Just Think About It

Thinking about a task ≠ doing the task.

Planning to plan ≠ progress.

Once you've broken your Big Task down into pieces, **put them into your Sketch Plan.** Spread them out. Don't try to do all the steps in one day. Space them through the week based on urgency, energy, and your other commitments.

Example Sketch:

Tuesday Mid-Morning Block (Deep Work)

Outline new workshop (1 of "Create new digital product")

Thursday Afternoon Block (Admin)

Upload files to product platform (4)

Saturday Flex Block

Write bonus lesson script (7)

That's three steps, done over six days. You're making consistent progress *without overloading yourself.*

6: Celebrate Each Micro-Win

Every time you complete a step—*no matter how small*—celebrate it.

- Cross it off
- Say "done!" out loud

- Tell a friend
- Put a gold star on your planner (yes, really)
- Eat a piece of chocolate
- Let yourself rest for five whole minutes without guilt

Because success isn't measured by how *fast* you climb the mountain.

It's measured by whether you keep putting one foot in front of the other.

And *every single counts.*

You Can Do Big Things—One Small at a Time

If you take nothing else from this section, take this:

It doesn't have to feel doable all at once. It just has to feel doable right now.

Big things are built in tiny, ordinary, five-minute chunks.

Sketch Planning gives those chunks a home.

You give them the momentum.

You don't need to conquer the whole thing today.

You just need to shrink the mountain into a molehill—one at a time.

And guess what? You're already doing it.

Setting Realistic Goals

Because burnout isn't a badge of honor, and "doable" is the new productive.

Raise your hand if you've ever made a list that looked something like this:

- Organize every room in the house

- Finally lose the baby weight
- Batch all your blog content for the next 6 months
- Meal prep every Sunday like a Pinterest mom
- Launch a brand new product
- Also: meditate daily, go to bed by 9, keep your house clean, and be emotionally available for everyone

...and then completely shut down by Wednesday.

Here's the thing: You don't need to dream smaller.

You just need to **dream smarter.**

Setting realistic goals is not about lowering your standards.

It's about creating goals that honor:

- Your current season of life
- Your energy levels
- Your mental load
- And the actual time you have (not the time you *wish* you had)

So let's talk about how to set goals that move you forward **without moving you into exhaustion**.

Why Unrealistic Goals Are So Tempting (and So Dangerous)

Setting massive, lofty goals feels good in the moment.

It gives you a little dopamine spike—a sense of control, of hope, of direction.

But when that "start a YouTube channel, reorganize the kitchen, and prep for the school fundraiser" goal list smashes into your actual life (appointments, grocery runs, sick kids, dog hair on the couch), the crash hurts.

And what often follows is guilt. Self-judgment. That inner voice saying:

"Why can't I stick to anything?"

"Everyone else seems to get it all done."

"Maybe I'm just not cut out for this."

Let's rewrite that narrative.

Unrealistic goals don't make you a visionary. They make you **stuck**.

Realistic goals, on the other hand? They *work*.

They give you wins. Build confidence. Create traction.

And that's what you need to stay motivated long enough to hit the finish line.

1: Assess Your Life Season with Honesty (Not Shame)

Before you write a single goal, stop and ask:

"What do I actually have capacity for right now?"

Are you in a **high-growth** season? (Excited, focused, ready to hustle?)

A **maintenance** season? (Keeping the ship afloat, doing what you can?)

A **recovery** season? (After burnout, illness, big life change?)

A **caretaker-heavy** season? (Young kids, elderly parents, mental load overload?)

An **in-between** season? (Where you're figuring it all out again?)

All of these seasons are valid.

But what works in one won't work in another. Trying to set high-output goals in a low-capacity season is a recipe for guilt—not success.

I've had seasons where "launch new course and run a summit" felt totally doable. And other seasons where my biggest win was getting through the week with clean laundry and semi-decent dinners. Both were real. Both mattered. Both required very different goals.

Sketch Planning Tip: Write down your current season *before* you goal set. Let it guide how much you take on.

2: Define Your "One Thing"

If you try to chase five goals at once, you'll end up feeling like you're spinning plates—and dropping all of them by week two.

Instead, choose **ONE main focus** at a time. This could be for:

- The month
- The quarter
- A 6-week sprint
- Or a single week if that's all you can manage right now

This doesn't mean you can't do *anything* else—it just means everything else is **secondary**.

Your main goal becomes the **anchor** of your Sketch Plan.

Examples:

- Focus Goal: Build and launch a digital product
- Support Tasks: Email newsletter, light housework, meal prep
- Focus Goal: Declutter and reset your home
- Support Tasks: Lower business commitments, pause new projects
- Focus Goal: Family connection and rest
- Support Tasks: Light content maintenance, say no to new obligations

This helps you say no (or *not now*) to all the other shiny ideas that want your attention. And that? Is how progress happens.

3: Break the Goal Down Until It Feels Kind

Let's take a goal like:

"Create and launch a course in 30 days"

That sounds exciting... until you realize how many steps it includes.

Instead of "launch course," break it into **micro-goals** like:

- Week 1: Outline course + decide on tech
- Week 2: Write lesson scripts + build templates
- Week 3: Record content + upload to platform
- Week 4: Write launch emails + share on social

Then take each week and break it into daily Sketch Plan Kings.

Monday King: Write 3 bullet points for Lesson 1

Tuesday King: Record intro video

Wednesday King: Upload + add workbook

Now you've got motion. Flow. Clarity.

You're no longer staring down a mountain—you're walking up the path.

4: Check Your Goal for These 3 Things

1. Is it specific?

"Get healthy" is too vague. "Drink 64 oz of water 5 days this week" gives you something clear to act on.

2. Is it measurable?

"Work on my blog" is hard to track. "Write 2 posts this week" lets you know if you did it.

3. Is it achievable in your current life season?

Be honest. If it feels like too much, it probably is. Shrink the goal instead of spiraling.

5: Build in Checkpoints + Flexibility

Realistic goals **adapt**.

Every week, review your Sketch Plan and ask:

- "Am I on track?"
- "Did life throw a wrench in things?"
- "Do I need to push this piece into next week?"
- "Is this still aligned with what I want?"

Goals can shift without being abandoned. You're not behind. You're in process.

Sketch Planning gives you built-in checkpoints. Use your review moments not just to plan—but to **pivot when necessary.** That's not failure—it's flexibility. And it's powerful.

6: Fuel Your Motivation with Wins, Not Pressure

Let's be real: some days, the only thing that got done was the one thing that *had* to. That doesn't make you lazy. That makes you human.

So instead of waiting until the end of the goal to feel proud, start **celebrating micro-wins** along the way:

- Completed a sketch? Win.
- Took one small step? Win.
- Rescheduled instead of quitting? Win.
- Rested on purpose? Win. (Yes, really.)

Motivation doesn't come from pressure.

It comes from momentum—and momentum is built on *tiny wins stacked over time.*

I used to think motivation meant getting fired up and pushing through. Now I know it's more about noticing how far I've come—even if it's just a baby on a messy day. That's what keeps me moving.

A Realistic Goal Honors Your Time, Your Energy, and Your Life

Here's what a realistic goal looks like:

- It fits into the time you actually have
- It adjusts when life shifts
- It creates pride, not pressure
- It builds momentum without burnout
- It feels *like you*—not like someone else's version of success

You can still build big things.

You can still dream wildly.

But now? You'll do it in a way that's sustainable, kind, and made for *real life*—not the fantasy version that lives on Instagram.

So go ahead. Sketch your next goal.

But do it with clarity. Compassion. And a little bit of coffee. (Decaf or not, you do you.)

Utilizing Rewards and Incentives

Because you're not a robot, and you deserve a little dopamine boost.

You've probably used rewards before—maybe for your kids, your students, your dog (no shame, they're very trainable), or even your spouse. But when was the last time you built a **real reward system** for *yourself*?

Here's the thing: Motivation doesn't just happen.

It needs fuel. And one of the best ways to fuel it—especially when a task feels boring, hard, or never-ending—is to pair it with something your brain *actually looks forward to.*

Enter: rewards and incentives.

Used well, they can help you:

- Start tasks you've been avoiding
- Stay focused when your energy dips
- Celebrate progress (not just perfection)
- Feel like you matter in the middle of all the chaos

So, let's talk about how to build your personal reward system—Sketch Planning style.

Why Rewards Work (Especially for Busy Women and Moms)

Let's be real: most of us are **doing a lot** for everyone else.

We cheer our kids on. We support our partners. We manage school calendars, snacks, birthdays, appointments, and *all* the behind-the-scenes stuff no one else sees.

And we often forget to cheer ourselves on.

But your brain? It craves acknowledgement. It *needs* that little hit of joy to stay motivated.

When we don't reward ourselves, we start to associate productivity with exhaustion and obligation. When we do reward ourselves, we create a healthy, positive connection between effort and joy.

My confession:

There was a time when I didn't let myself rest until *everything* was done. (Which, it never is.) Now I sketch in rewards like "watch a favorite show guilt-free" or "Starbucks treat if I finish the big task before noon." And I *actually look forward* to working through the plan. It's amazing how different it feels when your brain knows there's something good waiting at the other end.

1: Identify the Tasks That Need Incentives

Not every task needs a reward—but the ones you dread? The ones you've been putting off? Those definitely do.

Think about tasks that are:

- Emotionally heavy (filing taxes, tough emails)
- Boring or repetitive (admin work, folding laundry)
- Overwhelming (organizing photos, writing sales pages)
- New or unfamiliar (starting a blog, setting up tech)
- Long and focus-heavy (editing a course, planning a launch)

Ask yourself:

"What tasks drain me the most—and what little boost would help me follow through?"

2: Choose Meaningful Rewards (That Fit Your Season)

Your reward doesn't have to be big, fancy, or expensive. It just has to feel *good enough* to create positive anticipation.

Reward ideas:

- A hot/cold coffee you drink *before* it gets cold/warm
- 20 guilt-free minutes with your favorite show
- A walk alone with your podcast and no tiny humans
- A new notebook or candle
- A quiet scroll through your Pinterest boards
- A solo Target trip. With a cart. No list.
- A section of a book that has nothing to do with business, parenting, or self-improvement

This is about pleasure and restoration—not productivity.

Bonus Tip: For big goals, add *milestone rewards.*

Example: Finish recording 5 lessons buy new slippers. Launch product dinner out. It gives your brain little checkpoints to work toward.

3: Build Rewards into Your Sketch Plan

Make it visual and intentional.

In your plan, you might sketch:

- "Admin Hour: Inbox cleanout 20-min reading reward"
- "Finish 2 blog drafts walk and podcast block"
- "Pomodoro sprint x4 whiskey on the rocks (don't judge!)"

- "Laundry, vacuum, dishes guilt-free YouTube rabbit hole after"

You're not just "earning" the reward. You're **fueling the work** with it.

The best part? When you *see* that treat at the end of your Time Block, your brain is way more likely to show up and stay focused.

4: Let Yourself *Actually Enjoy It*

Here's the hard part for a lot of us high-achiever, people-pleaser, default-parent types:

You have to let yourself rest.

You have to *receive* the reward.

No guilt. No "I didn't do enough." No waiting until the next task is also done.

You did the thing. Celebrate it. Let it land.

Even if it wasn't perfect. Even if you moved slower than you wanted. Even if you had to reschedule twice before you got it done.

You still showed up. And that deserves a little joy.

What to Avoid with Rewards

Let's keep it helpful and healthy. Avoid:

- Rewards that punish ("I'll skip dinner until I finish this." Nope. You need food.)

- Rewards that pile on guilt ("I'll only watch TV if I finish EVERYTHING." That's a trap.)

- Overdoing it with things that sabotage your health or budget (we love Starbucks, but maybe not 6x a day)

- Skipping the reward because "I didn't earn it enough" (yes you did. take the win.)

The goal here is to **build trust** with yourself.

You set a plan. You follow through. You treat yourself with kindness.

That's a *huge* mindset shift.

You Deserve a Plan That Includes Joy

Too often, we build plans that are full of:

- Obligations
- Deadlines
- Chores
- Expectations
- ...and *zero joy.*

Then we wonder why we're exhausted, burned out, and completely unmotivated.

Sketch Planning is about **grace AND structure.**

It's about **effort AND ease.**

It's about **progress AND pleasure.**

Rewards are not an afterthought.

They're an essential part of staying in motion *without* losing yourself.

So go ahead—sketch in the coffee break. Plan the pedicure. Celebrate the two loads of laundry you actually folded *and* put away (honestly, heroic). You've earned it.

Seeking Accountability

Because following through is easier when someone's cheering you on (or kindly calling you out).

If you've ever said...

- "I'll start that project Monday."
- "Next week I'll get serious."
- "As soon as life calms down..."
- "I know what to do... I just don't *do* it."

...you're not lazy. You're not undisciplined.

You're just lacking one very human, very powerful ingredient: **accountability**.

And guess what? That's not a flaw—it's a signal. It means you're *normal.* We aren't built to live (or create, grow, or finish goals) in isolation.

We need support systems. Especially when we're juggling work, kids, dishes, mental load, creative ideas, emotional ups and downs, and—oh right—trying to grow personally or professionally, too.

So let's explore how **accountability** helps you move forward *without more pressure*—and how to build it into your Sketch Planning life in a way that feels light, loving, and totally doable.

Why Accountability Isn't Weakness—It's *Wise Strategy*

Somewhere along the way, a lot of us picked up the belief that needing accountability = failure.

"If I were really serious about this, I wouldn't need someone to check in on me."

"If I can't do it myself, maybe I'm not cut out for it."

NOPE. Let's shut that down.

Here's the truth:

People with accountability are 65% more likely to complete a goal.

Add regular check-ins? That jumps to 95%.

So yeah—accountability *isn't weakness*. It's **brain science**.

Your brain is wired to respond to:

- Deadlines
- Encouragement
- Shared vision
- External feedback
- Micro-rewards (like getting to say, "I did it!")

When you tell someone your plan, your brain treats it like a real commitment—not just a wish floating around your to-do list.

Real Life Example: Two Moms and a Weekly Walk

Let's say you and a fellow mom are both trying to grow your blogs.

You sketch time to write each week—but you keep bumping it for other things.

So you text her:

"Want to be accountability buddies this month? Let's check in every Monday. One goal, one win, one thing we need help with."

You both agree. Every Monday, you voice message each other with:

- Your King task for the week

- Whether last week's plan worked
- Any wins or challenges
- Your "I did it!" moment on Friday (even if it's tiny)

Now your blog post isn't just *your problem*. It's *a shared intention.*

When she says, "I'm proud of you for getting that done, even though this week was wild," it *lands*. It keeps you moving. You don't feel behind. You feel *in process*—and supported.

That's the magic.

Step-by-Step: Building Accountability into Your Sketch Plan Life

1: Decide *What* Needs Accountability

Not every task or goal needs it. But ask yourself:

"Where do I get stuck the most?"

"Which goals feel too big to manage alone?"

"What have I been saying I'll do forever... but haven't started yet?"

These are your accountability-priority areas.

Sketch Planning areas that benefit most from outside support:

- Business launches or digital product creation
- Health habits (like walking, water, or sleep)
- Decluttering or big home projects
- Sticking to your Focus King each week
- Creating content or staying consistent on a platform
- Implementing a routine you've been avoiding

Start small. One goal. One habit. One support system.

2: Find the *Right* Accountability Partner

This matters more than people think.

Great accountability partners:

- Understand what you're working toward
- Are reliable (even if they're not perfect)
- Can cheerlead AND give gentle nudges
- Respect your life season and capacity
- Don't project their goals or pace onto you
- Make you feel *seen*, not shamed

They might be:

- A business friend with similar goals
- A friend you trust deeply
- A coach or mastermind group
- A community you're already part of (even a DM check-in buddy!)

What matters most? That the connection feels safe and supportive—not performative or pressure-filled.

My Tip:

Start with one simple ask: "Want to check in with each other every Friday for the next 3 weeks? Just a 2-minute voice note to say what worked and what didn't."

That keeps it low-stakes, but so powerful.

3: Choose Your Accountability Format

There are *so* many ways to do this. Pick the one that fits your personality and lifestyle:

Casual Buddy Check-In:

- Weekly texts or voice messages
- Shared Trello board, Notion doc, or checklist
- "Reply to this thread when you've done your King today!"

Group or Partner Work Sessions:

- Co-working Zooms
- Focus sessions (Pomodoro-style)
- Voxer chat threads where everyone shares their progress

Sketch Planning Specific:

- Share your Focus King for the week with your buddy
- Send a photo of your Sketch Plan on Monday and Friday
- Host a "Sunday Sketch Together" Zoom with a friend

Make it visual. Make it fun. Make it *yours.*

4: Add Encouragement + Rewards

Accountability doesn't have to be all logistics.

Let it be fun, playful, and **motivational.**

Think:

- Send each other a GIF or funny meme when you complete your goal

- Create a shared "wins" doc where you both celebrate each milestone
- If you both hit your King goals, plan a mini reward together (ice cream, book swap, digital high five!)

It doesn't have to be deep. It just has to feel good.

What to Avoid in Accountability Partnerships

Here's the truth: not all accountability feels encouraging. And that matters.

Watch for red flags like:

- Partners who disappear without warning
- Overly critical or competitive tone
- Making you feel "less than" if you need to adjust your goals
- Constant comparison
- Shaming for needing flexibility

Healthy accountability sounds like:

"You've had a hard week. Want to shift your King to something more manageable?"

"You're doing great—this is hard stuff. I'm proud of you for sticking with it."

"No guilt. Let's just sketch the next together."

Support should *lighten* the load, not add to it.

You're Still in Charge—But You Don't Have to Go It Alone

You can do hard things.

You're already doing so much.

But that doesn't mean you have to keep carrying it all by yourself.

Accountability isn't about proving anything. It's about **receiving support** that reminds you:

- What you care about
- Why you started
- And that it's okay to need encouragement, consistency, and connection to follow through

So go ahead—open that text thread, reach out to the friend, post in the group.

Let someone in. Let them walk with you.

Sketch it. Share it. Show up—together.

You'll be amazed how far that little shift takes you.

12

Digital Sketch Planning: Utilizing

Integrating with Existing Calendars and Apps

Because your planner shouldn't live in one app while your real life is scattered across six others.

By now, you've got the foundation of Sketch Planning down:

Flexible time blocks.

Kings and Easily Moved {hanging) tasks.

Self-care and recovery space.

Adaptability when life gets loud.

But if your digital life still looks like this:

- Appointments in Google Calendar
- Grocery list in Notes
- Project tasks in Trello

- Reminders popping up randomly
- And your actual Sketch Plan... somewhere in your head (maybe?)

It's time to bring it all together.

Not by reinventing your system—but by creating simple, intentional *connections* between the tools you already use and your Sketch Plan.

This section is about *reducing friction*, not adding steps.

Let's show your readers how to integrate *lightly*, so their digital life supports their real one.

Why Integration Helps (and Why It Has to Be Simple)

Integrating your Sketch Plan with your other tools helps you:

- Stop re-entering the same tasks in multiple places
- Reduce mental clutter from bouncing between apps
- See your *whole life* in one flow
- Make sure your Kings don't get buried by random reminders or meetings
- Keep your Sketch Planning rhythm alive—even when you're in full "default mom mode"

But here's the golden rule:

If the integration adds stress, it's not worth it.

This is about ease, not overwhelm.

1: Pick Your Planning Hub

Where will your **main Sketch Plan live**?

Choose a central location that you enjoy using, such as:

- A digital planner in GoodNotes or Notability (if you're a handwriting fan)
- A custom dashboard in Notion or Trello
- A simple Google Doc or spreadsheet
- A printed weekly Sketch Plan page on your fridge (yep, that counts!)

The key is to have **one primary space** where you sketch each week's blocks and priorities. Then, everything else connects to *that.*

I sketch my week in GoodNotes using a reusable template. Then I check Google Calendar and Trello each morning to make sure what's scheduled still matches my real capacity. If it doesn't—I re-sketch. Easy.

2: Sync with Your Calendar (Without Getting Sucked Into It)

If you're using **Google Calendar**, **Apple Calendar**, or **Outlook**, try this:

- Color code your Time Blocks so they visually match your Sketch Plan (ex: Morning Block = Yellow, Self-Care Block = Blue)
- Add your fixed appointments (Zoom calls, school pickups, therapy, etc.)
- Use "all day events" or "reminders" to represent your **Focus King**
- If you want, create a "Sketch Plan" calendar layer just for your blocks

Pro Tip: Don't try to schedule *every single task* in your calendar. That defeats the flexible nature of Sketch Planning.

Use your calendar for *anchors*—things that *must* happen at a certain time—and keep the rest in your main Sketch Plan.

3: Connect Task Management Tools (Trello, Asana, Notion, etc.)

If you use a project or task manager, you can sync it to your Sketch Plan like this:

- Each week, review your task app for deadlines or to-dos
- Pull 1–3 top priorities into your **King section** for each day
- Leave the rest as "Easily Moved" or batch them into a Flex Block
- Don't copy *everything*—just what belongs in your *current* week

Example:

You've got 10 tasks in Asana for your blog launch. During your weekly sketch, you look them over and pull 2–3 into your Kings for the week. The rest stay in Asana, where they're safe and waiting—but not overwhelming your brain or planner.

4: Use Reminders and Notes Apps *Intentionally*

You're probably already using one of these:

- Apple Reminders
- Google Keep
- Todoist
- Evernote
- Simple Notes

These are great for:

- Storing Easily Moved tasks
- Capturing ideas before they fly away

- Logging future Kings or wish list projects
- Creating recurring task lists (like a weekly reset routine!)

Use them as your **brain extension**, but not your main planner. Think of them as:

"Holding spaces, not command centers."

Then once a week, scan them as part of your **Sunday Sketch Ritual** to pull what matters into your week.

5: Build a Weekly Integration Flow

Each week, you can create a 15–20 minute rhythm to bring everything together:

Your Weekly Sketch + Sync Flow:

1. Open your Sketch Planner
2. Check Google Calendar for fixed appointments
3. Scan Trello/Notion/Asana for top 3–5 tasks
4. Review Notes or Reminders for flexible tasks
5. Choose 1–3 Kings per day and sketch them into Time Blocks
6. Plug in self-care, rest, or buffer time (always!)
7. Leave white space for surprises + Flex Blocks
8. *Done!*

Optional: Take a screenshot or photo of your Sketch Plan and make it your phone lock screen for easy access all week.

Tech Is a Tool—Not the Boss

You don't need a full-blown digital system.

You don't need every app.

You just need a plan that matches your life—and a few simple ways to *connect* the pieces.

So pick your planning home.

Choose your tools.

And integrate just enough to make things flow better—not harder.

When done right, your apps will support your Sketch Plan—**not compete with it**.

Let them hold your chaos.

You focus on what really matters.

Utilizing Digital Features

Because if your phone is already glued to your hand, it might as well help you stay sane.

Let's be real: Tech can either make your life easier... or leave you with 38 open tabs, 12 notifications you forgot to check, and a weird sense of doom every time your screen lights up.

But here's the thing—when used intentionally, **digital tools can do the heavy lifting**.

From scheduling to remembering birthdays to reordering the dog food automatically, tech can free up your brain space so you can focus on what matters—like your kids, your content, or just eating a meal at mealtime.

In this section, we're going to make that happen.

Let's turn your tech into your **personal assistant**—the kind that doesn't need reminders or caffeine.

Why Use Digital Features?

You don't need more tools. You just need to use your **existing tools** more effectively.

Smart features can help you:

- Automate repetitive tasks
- Stay on top of due dates and priorities
- Keep everything in one place
- Reduce decision fatigue
- Create calm out of chaos (even with kids screaming in the background)

The goal? **Less remembering. More living.**

1: Use Smart Reminders (So Your Brain Can Relax)

Stop relying on memory for everything. You're not a robot. You're a legend who deserves digital backup.

Try This:

- Use **Apple Reminders**, **Google Tasks**, or **Todoist** to:
    - Set location-based reminders (ex: "Buy milk" pops up when you're near the grocery store)

  - Add recurring reminders for weekly tasks (pay bills, call Grandma, clean out lunchboxes)
  - Set time-based nudges for Easily Moved tasks ("Check email" at 2:30, when you're less fried)

My Tip:

I set a recurring Monday reminder to sketch my week. It pops up in the morning so I don't "accidentally" forget when Monday gets wild.

2: Automate Routine Scheduling

If you do the same tasks regularly, make them repeat automatically.

Tools like:

- **Google Calendar** (repeat events weekly/monthly)
- **ClickUp**, **Trello**, or **Asana** (recurring tasks, reminders)
- Even **Alexa** or **Siri** ("Remind me to clean out the fridge every Friday at 4 p.m.")

Don't manually plan what can plan itself.

Pro Tip: Create a "Sketch Routine Template" in your task manager that you copy each week. Add recurring Kings like content creation, appointments, school events, meal planning, etc.

3: Create Templates (Why Reinvent the Wheel?)

Templates are your time-saving BFFs. Use them for:

- Your **weekly Sketch Plan layout**
- Repeating **checklists** (blog post workflow, launch week, school supplies)
- **Daily routines** (AM/PM blocks, morning prep for kids, cleaning tasks)

Where to create/store templates:

- **Google Docs or Sheets**
- **Notion** pages
- **Trello/ClickUp/Asana** task templates
- **Canva** (for visual layouts)

My Tip:

I have a reusable "Launch Sketch Plan" template I duplicate every time I'm prepping a new product. It includes each broken into Kings and Easily Moved Tasks. Game. Changer.

4: Use Widgets and Lock Screens for Visual Planning

Your phone is the most checked item in your life. Let it work for you.

Try:

- A **calendar widget** that shows your top 3 priorities
- A **home screen shortcut** to your digital Sketch Planner
- A custom **lock screen** image of your plan (just screenshot it from GoodNotes or Notion!)
- A minimalist **to-do list widget** with your Focus King front and center

These tiny tools keep you anchored—without needing to open a single app.

5: Sync Across Devices (So You're Never Stuck)

We all move between laptops, phones, tablets, and even smart speakers.

Use tools that **sync automatically**, so you're never stuck thinking, "Where did I write that?"

Great sync-friendly options:

- **Google Keep**, **Apple Notes**, or **Notion**
- **Evernote** for idea storage and list-building
- **Dropbox** or **Google Drive** for accessing planning templates anywhere

Sketch Planning Tip: Store your template in the cloud and open it from wherever you are. Use a stylus on your iPad *or* type updates from your phone. Keep it flexible and fluid.

Bonus: Tech Boundaries Are Self-Care

Let's not pretend more tech = more peace.

Create tech boundaries so your tools serve you *without* taking over:

- Use **Focus Mode** or **Do Not Disturb** during your Focus Blocks
- Turn off non-critical notifications (you do not need to know when someone likes your IG Reel while you're trying to cook dinner)
- Schedule **"tech-free" Time Blocks**—even 30 minutes a day is powerful
- Keep your most-used apps for Sketch Planning *on your home screen*—and bury the distractions

Remember: You're the boss of your tech. Not the other way around.

Use Technology to Support the *Life You Want*

You don't need to be a digital expert.

You don't need five new apps.

You just need a few **smart, supportive features** that reduce the mental load and increase your clarity.

Let your tech:

- Remind you (so you don't forget)
- Repeat for you (so you don't redo)
- Store ideas (so your brain can rest)
- Show your plan (so you stay grounded)

It's not about doing *more*. It's about using what you already have *better*.

So give yourself the gift of *ease*. Sketch your week. Tap into those smart features.

And let your digital life feel *like it's working with you—not against you.*

Maintaining Data Security

Because if your entire week lives in the cloud, you want to make sure it stays safe and sound.

You've got your digital Sketch Planner set up.

You've got your time blocks, your Kings, your meal plans, your Zoom links, your life… all organized and flowing beautifully.

And then one day… your app crashes.

Or your phone takes a swim in the toilet.

Or your Google account gets hacked and locked.

Or your toddler thinks your iPad is a coloring book.

This section isn't here to scare you—it's here to empower you.

Let's make sure your beautiful Sketch Plan (and all your precious notes, checklists, and templates) are safe, secure, and recoverable no matter what happens.

Why Data Security Matters (Even for "Just a Planner")

Sure, your Sketch Plan might not contain bank info or classified documents. But it probably holds:

- Personal goals
- Business to-dos
- Family schedules
- Health appointments
- Passwords or sensitive information
- Workflow checklists you've poured hours into

Losing that isn't just inconvenient—it can be *devastatingly disruptive.*

So let's walk through how to keep your planning system **safe, synced, and backed up**—with minimal tech stress.

1: Choose Cloud-Based Tools with Automatic Sync

Whether you're using Trello, Notion, GoodNotes, or Google Docs, make sure your tools:

- **Back up to the cloud**
- **Sync across devices**
- **Auto-save your work frequently**

Why it matters: If you lose or break a device, you're not starting over. You're just logging in from somewhere else.

Look for tools that sync with:

- **Google Drive**
- **iCloud**
- **Dropbox**
- **OneDrive**

My Tip:

I keep all my templates in Google Drive and sync GoodNotes to iCloud. I can access my plan from any device, which has saved me more than once during unexpected chaos.

2: Use Strong Passwords + Two-Factor Authentication

This is the digital version of locking your front door.

- Use a **unique password** for your planner tool (not "123Sketch")
- Turn on **two-factor authentication (2FA)** wherever possible
- Use a secure password manager like **1Password** or **LastPass** to store login info

Pro Tip: If your Sketch Plan includes personal information, client details, or business tasks, 2FA isn't optional—it's essential.

3: Backup Regularly (Yes, Even If You Use the Cloud)

Cloud tools are reliable... until they're not. Things happen: apps glitch, accounts get locked, or you accidentally delete something.

Easy backup ideas:

- Export your Sketch Plan as a PDF weekly (for apps like Notion or GoodNotes)
- Create a **weekly backup folder** in Google Drive or Dropbox
- Email yourself a copy of your current plan
- Print a physical copy of your weekly block layout and Focus Kings (bonus: visual reminder on your desk!)

Sketch Planning Tip: Add a recurring "Backup Plan" Easily Moved task to your Sunday sketch session.

4: Secure Your Devices

You probably already do this, but let's double-check:

- Use a **passcode or biometric lock** on your phone and tablet
- Turn on **auto-lock** after inactivity
- Enable **Find My Device** (Apple or Android) in case your phone/tablet is lost or stolen
- Don't store sensitive info in unencrypted apps

And if you share a device with your kids, consider a **separate user profile** or app folder that keeps your planner safe from "accidental" edits.

5: Keep It Simple—But Private

Even if you're not planning nuclear launches, your schedule is **your life**. It deserves to be private.

Tips to protect your info:

- Avoid public Wi-Fi for syncing or logging into planning tools

- Don't share your planner links or files without password protection
- Use tools that let you **restrict editing** if collaborating (like sharing a view-only Notion page with a friend or team)

Real-life reminder: Your mental load is in your planner. You don't want it compromised—digitally or otherwise.

Bonus: Create a Simple "What If?" Plan

Yes, even this can be part of your Sketch Plan.

Create a mini emergency checklist:

- Where your backup files live
- Login info (securely stored!)
- A printed version of your week's top 3 priorities or Focus King
- A short list of what to do if your tech goes down (ex: "Text accountability buddy," "Use paper backup," "Recreate layout from last template")

This takes 10 minutes now and saves **so much stress** later.

Your Peace Is Worth Protecting

Sketch Planning is all about creating calm, clarity, and space in your life.

Let's protect that.

You don't need to be a cybersecurity expert.

You just need a few simple systems to make sure your digital world *supports you without putting you at risk.*

So:

- Back it up.
- Lock it down.

- Keep it private.
- Rest easy knowing your plan is safe.

Because your plan holds more than tasks—it holds your goals, your rhythm, your peace of mind.

And that's worth protecting.

13

Troubleshooting and Common Challenges: Addressing Obstacles

Overwhelm and Perfectionism

Because doing "all the things" perfectly is a great way to end up crying in your laundry pile.

We need to start with a little truth bomb:

Overwhelm and perfectionism don't come from being lazy.

They come from caring *too much*, trying to do *too much*, and believing that the only way to be "enough" is to be *everything*.

Sound familiar?

If you've ever:

- Rewritten a to-do list 3 times because it didn't *look right*
- Delayed a task for weeks because you wanted it to be "perfect"

- Said yes to one more thing even though your plate was already full
- Felt like a failure for needing rest
- Spiral-purchased organizing tools instead of just taking a break (guilty)

...then welcome. You're not alone. You're not broken.

You're just caught in the burnout triangle of **expectations, perfectionism, and pressure**.

Let's get out of that triangle together—using the Sketch Planning method as your flexible, kind support system.

What Is Overwhelm, Really?

Overwhelm happens when your *perceived demands* exceed your *perceived capacity*.

It's not just about how much you have to do—it's about how impossible it all feels, all at once. It turns your brain into static. You can't prioritize. You can't start. You can't breathe.

Cue:

- Task paralysis
- Snapping at your partner
- Crying over lost socks
- Procrastination masked as "planning"
- Suddenly deciding today's the day to clean the entire pantry

This isn't a failure of discipline. It's a sign your system needs **space and support**.

The Role of Perfectionism

Here's the twist: perfectionism *looks* like ambition or responsibility...

But it's actually **fear in a fancy outfit**.

Fear of:

- Being judged
- Falling short
- Disappointing people
- Not being good enough
- Failing (or worse, failing *publicly*)

So we do more. Try harder. Rewrite again. Delay until we can do it "right."

Perfectionism says, "It only counts if it's flawless."

Sketch Planning says, "It counts because you did what matters."

Let's shift toward that.

1: Know the Signs of Overwhelm + Perfectionism

Before you can manage them, you've got to recognize them.

Common signs:

- You keep adding things to your to-do list even as you check stuff off
- You avoid starting projects because they feel too big
- You over-research, over-plan, or wait for the "perfect time"
- You feel guilty taking breaks
- You beat yourself up for not "doing it right"

- You finish the day exhausted, unsure of what you even accomplished

My inner perfectionist loves to sneak in during "productive" moments. I'll sketch a beautiful plan and then suddenly feel like I have to *do it all right now.* That's not motivation—that's anxiety wearing lipstick. I've learned to pause, breathe, and ask:

"What's enough for today?"

2: Redefine "Enough" with Sketch Planning

Sketch Planning exists *because* life isn't linear or perfect.

It helps you shift from:

- "I have to finish this *perfectly* today"
- to "I'll sketch what matters and adjust with grace."

Instead of cramming 12 tasks into one block, try:

- Choosing a **Focus King**
- Sketching in **white space**
- Labeling tasks as **"optional"** or "bonus"
- Saying out loud: "If I do this one thing today, I won."

This re-trains your brain to see progress as success—not perfection.

3: Use Sketch Planning to Manage Expectations

Use your planner to:

- **Lower the daily task count** to 1–3 Kings max
- **Batch your Easily Moved tasks** so they don't fill every gap
- **Protect Rest Blocks** and treat them like real appointments

- **Visually mark your done items**—crossing it off gives your brain a dopamine hit
- **Move a King without shame** (it's called Sketch Planning, not Stone-Carving)

Try this language shift in your planner: Instead of: "I *have* to do all this today"

Write: "Here's what I *can* do today—and what can wait."

Your words matter. Your tone with yourself matters even more.

4: Break the Burnout Cycle Before It Breaks You

Burnout doesn't always arrive as a big crash. Sometimes it sneaks in like this:

- You're tired all the time, even after sleep
- You feel resentful of your own responsibilities
- You stop doing things that bring you joy
- You fantasize about running away to a cabin with no Wi-Fi

You can stop that spiral early by:

- Sketching in recharge time first
- Doing "just enough" intentionally
- Asking for help (before you collapse)
- Letting things be imperfect and still valuable
- Choosing calm over control

Real Talk: You Don't Need to Be Superwoman

No planner, no system—*not even this one*—will work if you believe your worth depends on being perfect.

Let me say it louder:

You are allowed to be messy and still be making progress.

You are allowed to say "this is enough for today."

You are allowed to sketch small and still feel proud.

Your value isn't in your productivity.

It's in your presence. Your resilience. Your *humanness*.

Sketch Planning gives you a way to live your life *on purpose*—not on pressure.

Done Is Better Than Perfect—and Peace Is Better Than Burnout

So, the next time you feel the urge to make your plan "just right"... pause.

Breathe.

Sketch lightly.

Start with what matters most.

Leave space for grace.

And remember—progress isn't ruined by imperfection.

It's built with small, imperfect steps that *still count*.

Let your Sketch Plan be your compass, not your critic.

You don't need to do more. You just need to do what *matters*—in a way that's sustainable, doable, and *kinder* to you.

You've got this.

Inconsistent Application

Because the goal isn't perfection—it's always coming back.

Let's just go ahead and normalize it: you will fall off the planning wagon sometimes. You'll forget to sketch your week. You'll skip a day, then maybe another. You'll feel "off" and convince yourself there's no point in planning because you've already messed it up. Then three weeks pass and your beautifully designed Sketch Plan is sitting in the digital shadows, gathering metaphorical dust while your brain goes back into overdrive.

Suddenly, you're juggling everything in your head again—mentally inventorying groceries while responding to emails, trying to remember who needs to be picked up where, and silently panicking over whether you missed a school theme day... again.

And this is when those nasty little thoughts start creeping in.

"Why can't I ever stick with anything?"

"I knew this wouldn't last."

"Maybe I'm just not a planner person."

Let's pause here.

Take a breath.

You are not broken. You are not lazy. You're not flaky, disorganized, or failing.

You're human. And this is part of the process.

Inconsistency doesn't mean your system doesn't work. It means you're living a full, unpredictable life—and you're doing your best. Some days your brain is fried, the energy's just not there, and sketching a plan feels like trying to build IKEA furniture with no instructions and a toddler climbing on your head. I get it. I've been there. Probably last Tuesday.

But here's what makes Sketch Planning different—it doesn't expect perfection. It welcomes you back, gently, no matter how long you've been gone.

You don't have to restart with an elaborate five-block layout and every King perfectly color-coded. Sometimes it's enough to scribble one Focus King on a sticky note and call it a win. Sometimes it's opening your planner and only jotting down "Rest," and that's more than enough. This method was made to flex with you, even when your motivation is at a solid 2 out of 10 and your energy is somewhere under the couch with the lost socks.

And the trick to finding consistency isn't doing it perfectly every single day. It's about always returning when you've wandered.

We often think that in order to stick with a habit, we have to do it flawlessly, every day, without skipping a beat. But that's not how habits are formed. They're not built through rigidity—they're built through rhythm. Through coming back. Through asking, "What's the *next* small thing I can do?" instead of "Why haven't I done *everything* already?"

This isn't a test you pass or fail. It's a practice. A tool. A gentle touchpoint to realign with what matters.

Motivation will come and go. Some days you'll feel energized and inspired to sketch your whole week and meal plan and map out a new product launch in the same sitting. Other days, you'll feel like all you can do is circle one King and hope it gets done before someone yells "Moooom!" from another room.

That's okay.

There is value in the quiet habit of showing up imperfectly. Of sketching *something*. Of sketching late. Of sketching halfway. Because all of those "less than perfect" moments? They're still building your rhythm. They still count.

And here's something you don't hear enough: your environment matters. If your planner is buried under a pile of unopened mail or lost in a sea of tabs on your laptop, you're less likely to reach for it. Out of sight really does mean out of mind. So make it visible. Make it inviting. Keep it where you'll bump into it—on your kitchen counter, as your lock screen, tucked next to your morning coffee spot. Let it become part of your space, not just your schedule.

And let's talk about your *why*. When the habit feels hard, when you just want to zone out and scroll instead of sketch, come back to that. Why are you planning in the first place? Is it to feel less scattered? To protect your time? To carve out space for yourself? To stop forgetting snack days?

Your why isn't just motivational fluff—it's the anchor that pulls you back when your brain tries to opt out. So write it down. Post it. Whisper it to yourself in the chaos. And remind yourself that returning to your plan—even after a long, messy break—is always worth it.

There is no "behind" in Sketch Planning. Just a new block. A new King. A new chance to come back.

You can forget your planner for a month and still return tomorrow.

You can sketch sloppily, half-heartedly, and still create peace.

You can have a whole week go off the rails and still choose to realign on Sunday.

It all still counts.

So next time you fall off—because you will (we all do)—don't waste time feeling bad about it. Just open your planner. Breathe. And sketch the next block.

Your plan is still here. Your time still matters. And you're still allowed to take the next imperfect forward.

That's not failure. That's *resilience*.

Welcome back.

Lack of Time

Because if your day feels like a speedrun, planning shouldn't be one more thing slowing you down.

If there's one universal truth among moms, multitaskers, and anyone with more responsibilities than free time, it's this:

"I would love to plan my week… if I ever had a minute to myself."

Let's be real—some days it feels like you barely have time to drink your coffee before it goes cold, let alone sketch out a thoughtful, strategic game plan for your day. Planning can *feel* like a luxury. One of those "someday when life slows down" things. But if we wait for life to slow down? We'll be waiting forever.

The truth is, the times when you feel like you *don't have time* to plan?

Those are the times you need your Sketch Plan the most.

Because you know what really eats up your time?

- Starting your day without a clue what's urgent
- Getting halfway through a task and realizing you forgot something more important
- Jumping between 17 little tasks because you don't know what the priority is
- Spinning your wheels with decision fatigue
- Having to redo things because they weren't planned or prepped in time

Those time leaks add up. And they leave you feeling drained before lunch. Sketch Planning doesn't make you immune to chaos—but it gives you *a structure that supports you through it.* And even better? It doesn't require hours of your week to make a big difference.

Sketch Planning works *because* it's efficient.

It's not about filling in tiny squares or assigning a job to every minute. It's about sketching the framework that gives your day direction—so you can stop wasting time wondering what to do next.

And no, it doesn't need to take 30 minutes. You can sketch a whole week in 10–15 minutes once you've got the hang of it. Even 5 minutes in the morning can completely shift your focus.

If you've been telling yourself you don't have time to plan, here's your gentle nudge: what if the plan is how you *get* time back?

It doesn't have to be some elaborate ritual. You don't need a desk full of pastel highlighters or 12 browser tabs open. You just need one quiet-ish moment, your planner (digital or paper), and the willingness to focus on *what matters most.*

Some weeks, that might mean sketching your blocks while sitting in your car before pickup. Other weeks, it might be scribbling your Kings on a sticky note while reheating leftovers. That's still planning. That still counts.

We tend to think planning has to look a certain way to be effective. But effective doesn't mean fancy. It means functional. It means helping you feel less scattered. It means giving you back mental energy. And it means not forgetting things like dress-up day, that meeting at 2, or the fact that you really do need to throw in that load of laundry before it becomes a science experiment.

So if time is tight, start small. Sketch one Time Block. Choose one King. Revisit your plan when you can. Add a note on your phone. It doesn't have to be a ceremony—it can just be a moment.

And if you're someone who craves structure but resists rigidity (hi, same), Sketch Planning is your sweet spot. You're not tied to a strict agenda. You're creating a flexible outline. A container. A map. You're not scheduling every second. You're simply saying: *here's what matters today, and here's when I'll do my best to honor it.*

When you keep your planning process simple, repeatable, and grounded in *real life*, it becomes sustainable. It becomes a rhythm, not a task. And like brushing your teeth or drinking water, it becomes something that supports your well-being without requiring a full mental download.

That's the goal. Not perfection. Not performance. Just progress that doesn't leave you feeling more behind than when you started.

So if you've been feeling too busy to plan, too tired to even try, this is your reminder: you don't have to do it all. You just have to do what matters. Sketch Planning helps you see that clearly—*quickly*—and then move through your day with more focus, more calm, and maybe, just maybe... enough time to drink your coffee while it's still hot.

Adapting to Change

Because life doesn't ask permission before it throws curveballs—and your plan should be able to bend without breaking.

If there's one thing you can count on as a human (and especially as a mom, caregiver, or creative), it's that no matter how beautifully you plan your day... something's going to show up and flip it on its head.

Maybe it's the school calling to say your kid isn't feeling well.

Maybe the internet goes out right before your client call.

Maybe you spill coffee on your planner or on your pants—or both.

Or maybe it's something bigger. A loss. An illness. A detour that shakes your rhythm at the core.

Change is inevitable. Interruptions are part of the deal. And while we can't stop them from happening, we *can* choose how we respond.

This section is about building resilience into your Sketch Planning practice—so when life zigzags, you don't feel like you've failed. You just *adjust.*

Because flexible planning isn't weak planning. It's the kind that actually works in real life.

Most traditional planning systems expect you to operate like a robot. You make the plan, you stick to the plan, you check the boxes, and you feel accomplished. But what happens when the dog throws up on the rug, the baby skips her nap, and the big project you thought you had two days to complete suddenly needs to be done by 3 p.m.?

In most systems, that means you're behind. Off track. "Failed" the day.

In Sketch Planning? That means you pivot.

You take a breath, you reassess your Kings, and you re-sketch the rest of the day or week based on what's now possible—not what you originally hoped would happen.

And here's the beautiful thing: the more you practice this flexible mindset, the more resilient you become. Not just in your planning, but in your actual life.

You begin to realize that one chaotic morning doesn't ruin your week.

That one forgotten task doesn't make you a failure.

That shifting your plan is not weakness—it's wisdom.

There's so much power in that.

When change hits (and it will), you don't have to white-knuckle your way through it. You don't have to cancel everything or throw the plan in the trash. You just need to pause and reframe.

What's still essential?

What can be moved, delayed, delegated, or dropped?

What's *actually* urgent, and what's just trying to feel that way?

Sketch Planning gives you permission to let go of what no longer fits—and make room for what *is*.

Maybe you planned to batch three work tasks today, but now you're navigating an emotional kiddo who needs extra snuggles and reassurance. Your plan bends to that.

Maybe your whole week was built around a product launch, and now your tech isn't cooperating. You pivot. You sketch new blocks. You preserve your peace in the process.

Resilience doesn't mean powering through without feeling anything.

It means honoring what's happening, and responding with intention instead of panic.

And here's a little mindset shift that can help:

You're not starting over every time your plan changes. You're continuing—just on a slightly different path.

That's all.

You haven't messed up. You're just adapting.

If your kid is home sick and suddenly you can't get anything done, that doesn't mean the week is ruined. You sketch what's possible. You name one Focus King. You shift the rest.

If your energy crashes midweek and you need rest more than productivity, you honor that too. Your Kings can move. Your blocks can stretch. And the world will keep spinning.

The goal isn't perfect productivity—it's a life that reflects your values, your energy, and your current reality. Especially when that reality changes on you without warning.

So when change comes—and it will—remember this:

You don't need to control everything to stay on track.

You just need the courage to adjust.

You don't have to pretend nothing happened.

You just need to re-sketch the next step.

And you're not failing when you change your plan.

You're succeeding at something far more powerful: staying present, grounded, and kind to yourself when it counts most.

Sketch Planning doesn't ask you to be perfect.

It invites you to be *real*.

To meet your life where it's at.

To pivot with grace.

And to know that whatever today looks like... you can start from there.

Lack of Time

Because you were never meant to do this alone—even if you're the one who usually figures it all out.

Let's get something out in the open: asking for help can be hard.

Especially when you're used to being the one holding it all together. You're the planner, the keeper of schedules, the one who remembers that Friday is "Crazy Sock Day" and that the dishwasher still needs unloading. You're the default, the go-to, the one-woman command center for your entire household or business.

And because of that, reaching out—for help, support, or even just someone to say "same"—can feel like weakness.

But it's not.

It's wisdom.

Because as much as Sketch Planning is a tool for self-leadership and clarity, **you are not meant to carry your world alone.**

Support is what makes consistency sustainable. It's what helps you return to your plan when you've drifted, or adapt when things shift, or even just stay encouraged when motivation dips. It's not about depending on others to do it *for* you—but allowing others to walk alongside you *while* you do it.

There's something incredibly powerful about being seen. About having someone say, "Oh girl, me too," when you admit you haven't sketched anything in days. About being in community with people who are trying to live more intentionally—not perfectly, just on purpose.

Support can look like a lot of things. It might be an accountability partner who texts you each Monday to remind you to sketch your week. It might be a friend who's also a mom, who swaps ideas and sanity-saving hacks. It might be a Facebook group or Slack channel or casual Voxer thread with a few biz besties who remind you that you're not crazy—just chronically interrupted.

Sometimes support looks like swapping childcare for an hour so you can focus.

Sometimes it's asking your partner to handle dinner while you sketch out your priorities.

Sometimes it's simply saying out loud, "Hey, I'm overwhelmed," and letting someone listen.

Other times, support comes from resources—things that extend your capacity when your own is running low. A podcast that grounds you. A printable that simplifies your planning. A video that reminds you to breathe. A template that gives you a head start instead of a blank screen.

And of course, sometimes support comes from within the Sketch Planning method itself. From the permission it gives you to not do it all. From the flexible structure that says, "You're allowed to change the plan." From knowing there's an entire mindset behind this—one that honors your capacity, protects your time, and doesn't expect you to function like a productivity machine.

Support is about setting yourself up for sustainability. For being proactive instead of reactive. For making it easier to keep going, especially when you'd rather crawl under a blanket and pretend nothing needs to be done.

And it's not just about the tough moments, either.

Support is what helps you celebrate the wins.

It's texting someone, "I did all my Kings today!" and getting the you deserve.

It's feeling like your progress matters—because someone else sees it too.

There's no gold star for doing everything by yourself. But there's a whole lot of peace, progress, and power in doing it *together*.

So go ahead—let people in. Ask for what you need. Share your process. Show up messy. Let your Sketch Plan be a bridge to connection, not just a tool for control.

The support you need might already be around you—you just haven't asked yet.

And if it isn't? You can create it. You can invite it in. You can start with one voice, one resource, one friend, one post that says, "I'm trying this thing—want to try it with me?"

You are not behind. You are not failing.

You're building something sustainable.

And you're allowed to let others support you as you do it.

Because success isn't about going solo.

It's about knowing when to lean in and who to lean on.

You're not weak for needing help.

You're smart for seeking it.

14

Embracing a More Organized and Less Stressed Life

Moving Forward with Purpose, Grace, and a Plan That Actually Works

Because the real success isn't in perfect planning—it's in moving forward with purpose.

Take a moment and look back—not just at this book, but at the journey you've taken alongside it.

Remember where you started. Maybe it was in a season of complete overwhelm. Maybe you were tired of trying to use planning systems that made you feel more behind. Maybe your days felt like one long game of mental ping-pong, bouncing between tasks, appointments, forgotten snacks, and half-finished thoughts.

And now... Things feel different. Not perfect. Not always predictable. But more manageable. More intentional. More you.

You've learned how to pause and sketch a plan that makes room for your real life. You've learned how to identify what actually matters, instead of drowning in what just feels urgent. You've practiced prioritizing your energy—not just your to-do list. And you've come to understand that planning isn't about control. It's about direction.

So what now? What does life look like when you carry this forward?

The beautiful thing about Sketch Planning is that it was never meant to end when you close this book. In fact, it's only just beginning. This isn't a rigid system with rules etched in stone. It's a rhythm. A mindset. A tool that meets you where you are and evolves as you do.

Looking ahead, you're not walking into a perfect future with a flawless system that guarantees nothing will go wrong. That's not realistic—and it's not the point. What you are walking into is a future where you feel better equipped to handle whatever comes. Where you're no longer reacting to your life, but responding to it with purpose and calm.

You'll still have off days. You'll still have weeks where the plan goes out the window. You'll still forget a school theme day here and there (because it's not humanly possible to keep up with pajama day, backwards day, bring-a-book day, and hat day... all in one month).

But you'll also return to your system with ease. Without guilt. With the confidence of someone who knows how to re-sketch, re-prioritize, and realign.

You'll have the ability to build out long-term projects using the same simple framework that keeps your laundry and meal planning on track. You'll move through launches, holidays, birthdays, and chaos with a steady sense of what matters most. You'll handle surprises with a plan that bends instead of breaks.

And here's something really exciting: Sketch Planning doesn't just help you survive the day. It helps you create the life you want. It opens up space to dream a little. To ask: What kind of days do I want more of? What do I want to protect time for? What am I always too exhausted to even think about—and how can I make room for that again?

Because now that you're not spending all your energy just holding things together, you finally have the capacity to build something new. More white space. More clarity. More moments of peace and pride in how you're showing up. More energy to pour into the things you love—your business, your family, your creativity, your friendships, or even just yourself. (Yes, you count too.)

Looking ahead, your Sketch Plan becomes more than a guide for the day. It becomes a reflection of your values. A tool for growth. A habit that grounds you in your season, whatever that season looks like.

You might evolve the layout. You might try digital or go back to paper. You might add stickers or keep it minimal. You might use your plan to prepare for a huge transition or just to make sure no one leaves the house without shoes. It all counts. It's all part of the journey.

And as life continues to shift—as it always will—you now have a steady hand to hold onto: your own. You've created something lasting here. Something flexible. Something powerful. And moving forward, that power stays with you.

You are not the same person who began this journey. You are more equipped, more centered, and far more capable than you likely give yourself credit for. You have proven that you can start again without shame. That you can sketch your way through the unpredictable, and that you don't have to be perfectly organized to be powerfully grounded.

So take this method. Make it your own. Sketch what's ahead. One week. One block. One breath at a time.

Because your life isn't meant to be perfectly planned. It's meant to be intentionally lived. And now you know how to do just that.

A Letter from Me to You

Hey friend,

First, let me just say—I'm proud of you.

You made it to the end of this book. Maybe you read it straight through, maybe you jumped around, maybe you skimmed parts. However you got here, *you got here*. And that matters.

When I first started creating the Sketch Planning method, it wasn't because I wanted another planner. It was because I *couldn't find one that worked for my life*. Everything out there felt too rigid, too complicated, or just didn't account for the mental load so many of us are carrying behind the scenes. I was tired of feeling behind before I even started my day. I needed something that gave me space to plan *realistically*, not idealistically.

So I made this. And now... you have it too.

This isn't just a method—it's a mindset shift.

It's a way to take back your time without burning yourself out.

It's the thing that reminds you: you can have structure and still have grace. You can be organized without being perfect. You can show up for your life without running yourself into the ground.

And the best part? You don't have to do it all.

You just have to do *what matters most.*

That's what Sketch Planning helps you figure out.

I hope this system helps you breathe a little easier.

I hope it gives you clarity when things feel chaotic.

I hope it lets you focus on your people, your work, your rest—without dropping your own needs to the bottom of the list again.

But more than anything, I hope it reminds you that you're doing better than you think.

Even on the messy days. Even when your plan falls apart. Even when you're sketching with a crayon on the back of a grocery receipt because that's all you've got.

It still counts.

You still count.

So as you move forward—into your next season, your next week, or even just your next block—I want you to remember this: You don't have to have it all together. You just need a plan that gives you room to *be human.*

You've got that now.

And you've got me, cheering you on from the other side of the page.

Cheers,

JESSICA

P.S. Don't forget to celebrate yourself. Often. Loudly. Even for the smallest wins. Especially for the smallest wins.

ENDNOTES

While the Sketch Planning method is an original framework developed from my personal experience and years of working with real-life moms and entrepreneurs, the following books, tools, and concepts have helped shape the way I think about time management, habit building, and intentional living.

Books & Authors

- Brown, Brené. *The Gifts of Imperfection: Let Go of Who You Think You're Supposed to Be and Embrace Who You Are.* Hazelden Publishing, 2010.
- Clear, James. *Atomic Habits: An Easy & Proven Way to Build Good Habits & Break Bad Ones.* Avery, 2018.
- Cirillo, Francesco. *The Pomodoro Technique.* FC Garage, 2006.
- Keller, Gary, and Jay Papasan. *The ONE Thing: The Surprisingly Simple Truth Behind Extraordinary Results.* Bard Press, 2013.
- McKeown, Greg. *Essentialism: The Disciplined Pursuit of Less.* Crown Business, 2014.
- Adachi, Kendra. *The Lazy Genius Way: Embrace What Matters, Ditch What

Doesn't, and Get Stuff Done. WaterBrook, 2020.

- Northrup, Kate. *Do Less: A Revolutionary Approach to Time and Energy Management for Ambitious Women.* Hay House, 2019.
- Robbins, Mel. *The 5 Second Rule: Transform Your Life, Work, and Confidence with Everyday Courage.* Confidence Project Press, 2017.
- Gilkey, Charlie. *Start Finishing: How to Go from Idea to Done.* Sounds True, 2019.

Concepts Referenced

- Eisenhower Matrix (adapted from President Dwight D. Eisenhower's urgent/important prioritization strategy)
- Time Blocking (widely popularized by Cal Newport, among others)
- Habit Stacking (as presented in *Atomic Habits* by James Clear)
- The Pomodoro Technique (created by Francesco Cirillo)

Additional Inspiration

- Mindfulness practices inspired by the work of Jon Kabat-Zinn and Tara Brach
- Digital organization strategies via tools like Notion, Trello, and Google Calendar

About the Author

J.D. Evans is a mom, creative entrepreneur, and professional chaos manager who believes planning should feel possible—not punishing. After spending way too much time trying to squeeze her real, messy life into rigid planner boxes, she developed Sketch Planning, a flexible, grace-filled method that helps moms manage their time without losing their minds.

She's the founder of Follow My Arrow, Launch Hub, and cohost of the (occasionally paused but always loved) She's Got It Together podcast. Jessica is all about helping women simplify their schedules, focus on what really matters, and finally feel like they're doing enough—because spoiler alert: they are.

When she's not sketching out time blocks or organizing launch plans, you'll find her laughing with her family, quoting movies with her husband, or enjoying a well-deserved bourbon on the rocks after a long day of life-ing.

www.ingramcontent.com/pod-product-compliance
Lightning Source LLC
Chambersburg PA
CBHW061557120626
46550CB00004B/1517
9798998669408